T0328191

Cambridge Elements ≡

Elements in Forensic Linguistics
edited by
Tim Grant
Aston University
Tammy Gales
Hofstra University

FORENSIC LINGUISTICS IN THE PHILIPPINES

Origins, Developments, and Directions

Marilu Rañosa-Madrunio
University of Santo Tomas

Isabel Pefianco Martin
Ateneo de Manila University

CAMBRIDGE
UNIVERSITY PRESS

Shaftesbury Road, Cambridge CB2 8EA, United Kingdom

One Liberty Plaza, 20th Floor, New York, NY 10006, USA

477 Williamstown Road, Port Melbourne, VIC 3207, Australia

314–321, 3rd Floor, Plot 3, Splendor Forum, Jasola District Centre,
New Delhi – 110025, India

103 Penang Road, #05–06/07, Visioncrest Commercial, Singapore 238467

Cambridge University Press is part of Cambridge University Press & Assessment,
a department of the University of Cambridge.

We share the University's mission to contribute to society through the pursuit of
education, learning and research at the highest international levels of excellence.

www.cambridge.org
Information on this title: www.cambridge.org/9781009107945

DOI: 10.1017/9781009106078

First published 2023

A catalogue record for this publication is available from the British Library.

ISBN 978-1-009-10794-5 Paperback
ISSN 2634-7334 (online)
ISSN 2634-7326 (print)

Forensic Linguistics in the Philippines

Origins, Developments, and Directions

Elements in Forensic Linguistics

DOI: 10.1017/9781009106078
First published online: March 2023

Marilu Rañosa-Madrunio
University of Santo Tomas

Isabel Pefianco Martin
Ateneo de Manila University

Author for correspondence: Marilu Rañosa-Madrunio, mrmadrunio@ust.edu.ph

Abstract: This Element offers a critical review of forensic linguistic studies in the Philippines. The studies within, collected over a period of eight to nine years, reveal relevant themes from texts in courtroom proceedings, legal writings, and police investigations. The studies also delve into issues of language choice and language policy. The Element begins with a description of language policy in the Philippines, focusing specifically on language in the legal domain. The main body of the Element is a critical review of Philippine forensic linguistic studies. This critical review takes a sociolinguistic stance, in that issues of language and law are discussed through the lens of social meanings and social practice. From this critical review of forensic linguistic studies, the authors hope to chart future directions for forensic linguistic studies and research in the Philippines.

Keywords: forensic linguistics in the Philippines, Philippine forensic linguistic studies, language in the legal domain, language and law interface

ISBNs: 9781009107945 (PB), 9781009106078 (OC)
ISSNs: 2634-7334 (online), 2634-7326 (print)

Contents

Series Preface

The Elements in Forensic Linguistics series from Cambridge University Press publishes across four main topic areas: (1) investigative and forensic text analysis; (2) the study of spoken linguistic practices in legal contexts; (3) the linguistic analysis of written legal texts; and (4) explorations of the origins, development, and scope of the field in various countries and regions. *Forensic Linguistics in the Philippines: Origins, Developments, and Directions* by Marilu Rañosa-Madrunio and Isabel Pefianco Martin provides our first Element in the last of these categories.

Madrunio and Martin are significant figures in bringing forensic linguistics to the Philippines and in this Element they describe and evaluate the progress of the discipline from their first attendance at the International Summer School in Forensic Linguistic Analysis in 2012, held in Malaysia, to the development of research and teaching largely through work at the University of Santo Tomas (UST) Department of English. A decade after the Malaysia summer school, with the publication of this Element they also look forward to hosting the International Association for Forensic and Legal Linguistics' biennial conference in July 2023.

Early on in establishing the Cambridge Elements in Forensic Linguistics series, Tammy Gales and I decided that we wanted to include a sub-series which would reflect the rise of the discipline around the world and this will be the first of these *Origins* Elements in our broader series. We are particularly delighted that in the first of these Elements, the spotlight is turned on an area of the world where forensic linguistics is relatively new rather than well developed. As the discipline grows and spreads, it is likely that it is from these areas that we will find not only growth but also real innovation in the application of linguistics to forensic texts and contexts.

We have future *Origins* Elements contracted for both Australia and China, and we look forward to receiving proposals from any country or region where forensic linguistics as a discipline is well established or just starting out.

Tim Grant
Series Editor

1 Introduction

Forensic linguistics (FL) as an interdisciplinary, multidisciplinary, and trans-disciplinary area of study extends its reach to domains outside linguistics alone. The discipline of FL is specifically concerned with language in legal systems, including all issues in which there is an interface between language and law. These include disputes on authorship, courtroom discourse, trademark protection, speaker identification, text authenticity, textual fraud and deception, comprehensibility of legal writings, and similar concerns in forensic contexts. Issues of FL also touch on language choice, language policy, issues of social justice, and inclusivity.

The field of research of FL in the Philippines is in its infancy. Fewer than ten years since it first attracted serious attention in education and research, FL has become a subject of growing interest in many universities in the country. Studies conducted in this area have since been published, with several more studies that are forthcoming. To date, there is already a critical mass of research undertakings on FL in the Philippines. Interesting areas of study have emerged and continue to do so as young researchers become motivated to venture into this field.

This Element offers a critical survey of FL studies in the Philippines. The studies, which represent research over a period of eight to nine years, reveal relevant themes from texts concerning courtroom proceedings, legal writings, and police investigations. The studies also delve into issues of language choice and language policy. The Element begins with a description of language policy in the Philippines, focusing specifically on language in the legal domain. The main body of the Element presents a critical survey of Philippine FL studies. This critical survey takes a sociolinguistic stance by positioning issues of language and law through the lens of social meanings and social practice. This Element concludes by charting future directions for FL research and practice in the Philippines.

The next section discusses significant concerns that need to be addressed by the government in relation to the language used in the field of law. It describes the linguistic diversity in the country, the issues that have emerged from current language/education policies, as well as the dim prospects for resolving such pressing issues over the coming decades.

2 Language in the Philippine Legal Domain

In the Philippines, language issues have often been contentious and controversial. This may be attributed to the fact that the country is one of the most multilingual and linguistically diverse nations in the world. The Philippines is home to about 185 individual languages; globally, it occupies the twenty-fifth rank among the most linguistically diverse nations, with a score of 84 percent in the Greenberg Linguistic Diversity Index (Lewis et al., 2016). Such linguistic ecology is further validated by the reality that virtually every Filipino can speak at least two or three different languages. These include their mother tongue, the national language of Filipino, and English, a colonial language that has been embraced and developed by Filipinos into a language of their own.[1] However, despite this rich linguistic repertoire, to what extent have multilingualism and linguistic diversity been appreciated in language policies? In the domain of law, how have language policies and practices addressed the need to be inclusive of Filipinos who are not knowledgeable about English, which is the dominant language in national legal practice?

The 1987 Philippine Constitution (Article 14, Section 6) mandates that the Filipino language is "a medium of official communication and language of instruction in the educational system." The Constitution also states (Article 14, Section 7) that "for purposes of communication and instruction, the official languages of the Philippines are Filipino and, until otherwise provided by law, English." Thus, even as there is a constitutional promotion of the national language, the law also points to English as a language of vital importance in Philippine society. To this day, English remains the dominant language in official communications in government, in trade and commerce, and in legal proceedings and transactions.

It should be pointed out that the Filipino language remains an important lingua franca in the country. The large number of speakers of this language may be attributed to its entrenchment in the lives of Filipinos through mass media. The decision to adopt a national language was formalized only in 1935 during the American colonial period. At that time, the Philippine Constitution of 1935 mandated that "Congress shall take steps toward the development and adoption of a common national language based on one of the existing native languages" (Article 14, Section 3). The language itself was not yet named. The process for selecting this national language from among the many Philippine languages was, as linguist Br. Andrew Gonzalez, FSC pointed out, "fraught with problems that only time can solve" (Gonzalez, 1996, p. 223). Speakers of the five most dominant Philippine languages, namely, Tagalog, Cebuano, Ilocano, Hiligaynon, and Bikol, engaged in seemingly endless arguments and debates. In the end, lawmakers opted to base the national language on Tagalog, the language of the ruling elite who reside in the political center of Manila. Thus, from a linguistic standpoint, Tagalog and Filipino are the same languages in structure.

It was in 1973 that Filipino was formally named as the national language, through a provision of the Philippine Constitution. Previous to this, the language was referred to as *Pilipino*. The shift to its present reference as *Filipino*

---

[1] For studies on English in the Philippines, see I. P. Martin (2020). Philippine English. In K. Bolton, W. Botha, & A. Kirkpatrick (Eds.), *The handbook of Asian Englishes*. Wiley Blackwell; and I. P. Martin (2019). Philippine English in retrospect and prospect. *World Englishes*, *38*(1–2), 134–143. https://doi.org/10.1111/weng.12367.

was brought about by efforts to present the national language as inclusive of all the other Philippine languages. It should be recalled that the speakers of other Philippine languages had earlier objected to the selection of Tagalog as the basis for the national language. In Filipino, the national language is imagined to integrate lexicon from other Philippine languages, hence its intended inclusivity. Over the years, Tagalog-based Filipino spread throughout the archipelago and has become a stable lingua franca in the country. However, despite its widespread use as a lingua franca, the language remains at the margins of important domains of society. Perceptions that Filipino is not a fully developed language persists. One domain that continues to resist the use of the national language is the legal system.

If language issues in the Philippines tend to be contentious and controversial, the place of English in the legal setting is even more problematic. Despite studies that have revealed the disadvantages of using English in various domains, English remains the dominant language in the Philippine legal domain. Martin (2012) underscores this in exposing the nonuse of Filipino and other local languages in courtroom trials, arguing that "the Filipino masses … depend on this legal system that continues to confound them, while frustrating attempts to gain genuine redress of grievances and uphold people's rights" (p. 12). Rañosa-Madrunio (2013) argues that if a judicial system employs English, legalese takes its place in the legal process. While legalese in legal discourse is expected, in contexts such as the Philippines, legalese in English only heightens the disparity between the English-knowing interrogators and the English-deficient interrogated. Most countries in Asia have been using their mother tongues in legal proceedings, but the Philippines continues to rely heavily on English (Powell, 2012). This is despite the fact that a large majority of participants in legal processes belong to the lower economic classes who are likely to receive less exposure to the English language, together with lower-quality English-language instruction.

In contrast to language policy in the legal domain, education policy in the country has already begun to seriously address the marginalization brought about by the English language. This was done through the institutionalization of Mother Tongue Based Multilingual Education (or MTB-MLE) in 2009, which was later enacted into law in 2013. Previous to MTB-MLE, basic education students were schooled in the Bilingual Education Policy (BEP), which required the use of English and Filipino only. This policy, which was in place for almost thirty years, did not contribute significantly to improving the learning outcomes of Filipino schoolchildren. In fact, the BEP was found to have contributed more to the deterioration of student progress because a large majority of Filipino students did not have functional knowledge of English. High dropout rates in schools were attributed to the fact that students could not understand their teachers. Because of this, the Department of Education introduced MTB-MLE, which allowed teachers to draw from the students' linguistic repertoire, their mother tongues, in order to learn. In contrast, the legal domain remains a stronghold of English. Laws and court decisions are largely written in English, and these are rarely translated into the national language, Filipino.

In order to expedite the processing of cases, the Supreme Court in 2007 directed trial courts in Bulacan, a Tagalog-speaking province north of Manila, to conduct court proceedings in Filipino only, thus launching the 2007 Bulacan Experiment. This move was a recognition by the Supreme Court that English represented a language barrier in the courtrooms. However, the experiment may be considered to have failed in that only one court persisted in the practice of using Filipino in trials. This may be attributed to the challenges faced by the stenographers who could not adjust to *Ikilat*, which is Filipino stenography. Soon after the launch of the project, judges and stenographers petitioned the Supreme Court to reconsider its directive, to which the Supreme Court acceded. Only one court maintained its Filipino-only policy, and this was Branch 80 of Malolos, Bulacan, which was at that time under the helm of Presiding Judge Ma. Resurreccion Ramos-Buhat. With the untimely demise of Judge Buhat in 2012, the practice of using Filipino only in court trials also ended (Martin, 2012).

Legal stakeholders themselves are not convinced that local languages have roles to play in the legal domain. In a survey on access to court justice conducted by the Social Weather Station (SWS) in 2003–4, a large majority of the lawyers and judges surveyed disagreed about the use of Filipino and other Philippine languages in the courts (SWS, 2005). This finding was reinforced by Martin's (2012) interviews with Visayas-based lawyers, who mostly believed that local languages would not thrive in the legal system. Most of these lawyers pointed out that extensive work must first be done to find equivalences of English legal terminology in Philippine languages. In addition, Filipino lawyers have been educated in English and would most likely find the use of non-English languages too challenging in both courtroom hearings and legal writing. With the diversity of languages in the Philippines, legal stakeholders might not be able to converse in other Philippine languages, let alone argue using these languages in a court of law. Thus, it appears that not much could be done as regards changing the language(s) of the law in the country or even providing spaces for local languages. Despite the notable attempts to introduce Filipino into the judicial system, the predominant lack of support from legal stakeholders makes the language situation in the legal domain seemingly hopeless.

In this section, we have presented the language situation in the Philippines, focusing specifically on language in the legal domain. We have demonstrated that English remains the language of choice among legal stakeholders, not only because this is the official language identified in policy documents, but also because of the perception that no other Philippine language can seem to fit the bill. In the next section of this Element, we will provide a critical survey of developments in Philippine FL studies, examining almost thirty FL research studies conducted over the last decade.

3 Developments in Philippine Forensic Linguistic Studies

This Element on the origins, developments, and directions of FL studies in the Philippines should ideally begin with the so-called ground-zero study that inspired other studies on the interface between linguistics and law. Linguistics in the Philippines has mostly focused on applied linguistics, with a large body of studies mainly on language pedagogy and education. Studies identifying themselves as FL research only began to be published in 2013 after a group of four Philippine academics were trained at the 2012 International Summer School in Forensic Linguistic Analysis (ISSFLA) held in Malaysia. This being the first such training event in Asia, it allowed these academics to bring their newly acquired knowledge and skills back to Manila.[2] However, a few studies published prior to the 2012 ISSFLA training in Malaysia may also be considered as FL studies, and these are included in this critical survey. In total, this Element surveys twenty-seven studies that may be categorized according to two strands: (1) analyses of language as deployed in legal processes, and (2) analyses of the language of legal texts. Table 1 presents a summary of these studies and their focus.

Among the early studies focusing on the interface between linguistics and law is that of Castro (1997), which analyzed the cognitive structuring of

---

[2] The University of Santo Tomas (UST) Department of English has been very active in promoting FL in the Philippines. The university has been offering the course "Forensic Linguistics" in its graduate program since 2014 and "Language and Law" in its BA English Language Studies Program since 2018. To complement its academic program offerings, the university, through its Department of English and the Graduate School, hosted the 2nd Asian Regional Conference of the International Association of Forensic Linguists (IAFL) and the 12th International Summer School in Forensic Linguistic Analysis (ISSFLA) in 2016, as well as the 1st International Conference on Forensic Linguistics in the Philippines in 2021. It also hosted monthly webinars on the different areas of FL from August 2020 to May 2021. More researchers from the university have presented their FL studies at international conferences since 2015. Some of their research outputs have been published in local and international peer-reviewed journals. In July 2023, the University of Santo Tomas will host the 16th IAFLL Biennial Conference in Manila. Additionally, the university has been teaming up with the national police and government judicial bodies to conduct training programs for police and court judges. Currently, a national professional organization on FL is being organized. It will be initially composed of language specialists, academics, legal and judicial professionals, police investigators, and other professionals who have a serious interest in FL.

Table 1 Summary of Philippine forensic linguistic studies.

Focus of analyses	Corpus	Number of studies
Language in legal processes	Transcripts of court proceedings	12
	Court decisions	4
Language of legal texts	Public policy, legal provisions	2
	Legal contracts	5
	Product warnings, patient information	4
Total number of studies		27

criminal appeal cases in the Philippines. In this study, the researcher hoped to "bring to the fore the interplay between the text and the various linguistic, sociolinguistic, and psycholinguistic factors" (p. 85) that provide structure to the cases. Although legal cases are usually expected to conform to a preferred pattern or logical sequence in the moves used, it was argued that appeal cases may have a different set of features, hence the choice of appeal cases for the corpus of the study. In this study, Castro underscored the need to approach legal texts as having a cognitive structure, or "the way by which members of a legal community write the way they do because they are influenced by the shared linguistic, sociolinguistic and psycholinguistic conventions they practice so that the texts they produce exhibit specific discoursal and organizational character-istics and patterns" (Castro, 1997, p. 87). The corpus of the study included seventy-four Philippine criminal appeal cases from 1974 to 1990. The mode of analysis, which used Bhatia's (1983) cognitive structuring model, focused on the choices made by the judge as writer in making known their intention. This model uses a four-move structure: (1) Identifying the case, (2) establishing the facts of the case, (3) arguing the case, and (4) pronouncing judgment. The third move, arguing the case, has three sub-moves: (1) Stating the history of the case, (2) presenting arguments, and (3) deriving *ratio decidendi* (Bhatia, 1983). By revealing the underlying cognitive structure of the legal texts, Castro attempted to describe the communicative functions of obligatory and optional moves.

Castro's work may represent the first attempt of a Philippine linguist to investigate the language of legal proceedings using linguistic tools. It is notable that the goal of the study was to eventually facilitate the comprehension of legal texts by nonlawyers or law students, hence its publication in a journal on teaching English for Specific Purposes (ESP). The hope was that awareness of the cognitive structuring of legal texts may pave the way for "developing easification procedures" (Castro, 1997, p. 104) for the development of English for Academic Legal Purposes (EALP). However, knowledge of cognitive structuring alone does not guarantee better comprehension of legal texts or influencing the "easification" of legal writing. The study stops at describing the cognitive structuring of the texts and its communicative functions without extending the argument to strategies for ensuring easification, and thus better comprehension of these legal texts. Bhatia (1983) presents easification as different from simplification, in that the former aims at "making a text more accessible to the learner, not by modifying its content or form but by developing in him specific strategies considered essential for that task" (p. 46). In ESP contexts, which Castro hoped to target, a discussion of these strategies for easification would have contributed tremendously to the community the study aimed to serve.

Another early study on the language of legal processes is that of Brylko (2002), employing two different sets of corpora, ten of which were decisions of Philippine appeal cases taken from Supreme Court Reports Annotated (SCRA) and another ten of which were American appeal cases taken from Lex Libris, an electronic collection of US Supreme Court decisions. Replicating Castro (1997), the two sets of corpora were compared and analyzed using Bhatia's (1983) model of cognitive structuring in legislative writing.

Careful examination of the cognitive structure of legal decisions in judicial settings revealed that both sets of data exhibited the same obligatory parts: (1) History of the case, (2) appeal proper, and (3) decision on the appeal. The sequence of these parts was likewise fixed. However, it was in the sub-moves where differences could be identified. For instance, in the Philippine sample, it can be noted that the decisions contained a very detailed presentation of the facts of the case, while the US sample only briefly presented the facts of the case. Overall, a marked similarity is recognizable in terms of cognitive structure. This demonstrates that members of the legal discourse community share a certain set of communicative purposes that dictate the style, structure, content, and intended audience of legal discourse.

Brylko's (2002) study set out to promote the importance of analyzing legal decisions, most especially those that are difficult to understand. Legal decisions also benefit teachers of legal English as they expose students to the discourse structure of criminal appeal cases, which may pave the way for easier under-standing of the vocabulary in legal cases. An interesting point to consider in this article is the fact that it intersects with other research areas such as world Englishes, contrastive rhetoric, and discourse analysis. Although it was a replication of Castro (1997), Brylko's study expanded the methodology by comparing legal documents in two established varieties of English. It validated the findings of Castro (1997) conducted at least six years earlier. Both Brylko and Castro cited the pedagogical implications of their studies for students of EALP in relation to the discourse structure of appeal cases, which is clearly pedagogical and academic in nature.

Since awareness of FL as an area of study in the Philippines began only after 2012, these studies by Castro in 1997 and Brylko in 2002 may be considered as products of their time, undertaken in the context of the need to promote studies on ESP rather than to contribute to linguistic studies of legal documents.[3] For Castro (1997), raising awareness about the cognitive structure of legal texts may facilitate better understanding of these texts. Brylko (2002) called for the introduction of authentic and unsimplified materials to learners of legal English at an appropriate level, at a point when the learners are prepared to handle the materials.

In contrast to the studies reviewed above, one early study on the linguistics of court proceedings did not extend its investigation to ESP and language learning. Santos's (2006) pragmatic linguistic analysis of triadic verbal exchanges among lawyers, court interpreters, and witnesses is noteworthy in underscoring the context of multilingualism in Philippine legal practice. The corpus of the study consisted of thirteen criminal cases in Zamboanga City, the Philippines, which analyzed lexico-semantic choice, syntactic question forms, as well as questioning patterns and strategies of lawyers during courtroom interrogation. The study was also interested in the interpretative strategies used by court interpreters in conveying lawyers' questions and witnesses' answers. The findings revealed that the modal auxiliaries *can* and *could* (as interpreted from the local language) were most frequent in direct examinations and were used as softening devices or as indirect requests by lawyers. Nominals of address such as *Mister/Sir* and *Miss/Madam* were employed equally by both prosecution and defense lawyers. Regarding the syntactic structure of questions, it was found that direct examinations were characterized mostly by *wh-* questions, followed by yes–no bi-polar questions or tag questions. Meanwhile, open-ended questions were hardly used by either prosecution or defense lawyers. Finally, on the interpretative strategies, the study revealed that self-repair strategies were predominantly employed by court interpreters; they were also found to frequently recast lawyers' questions or witnesses' answers to ensure that their messages were correctly conveyed to either party. Self-repair strategies came in the form of repetition or reformulation or a combination of both, thus underscoring the vital role of court interpreters in mediating communication in court proceedings.

---

[3] The popularity of ESP among Filipino English-language teachers is described in I. P. Martin (2014). English language teaching in the Philippines. *World Englishes*, *33*(4), 472–485.

Santos (2006) anchored the premise of the study upon the prestige status of English in the Philippines and how this has "uprooted [participants of courtroom trials] . . . from their natural and informal speech community to participate in a formal and highly conventionalized speech event" (p. 28). This prestige has even greater impact in a setting such as Zamboanga City, where the criminal cases are set, and where litigants do not normally use English in their everyday lives. Santos stressed the crucial role that court interpreters play in Philippine courtroom practice. The participants of the courtroom hearings were multilingual speakers of at least the dominant languages in the region, namely, Chavacano, Cebuano, and Tausug. However, one interesting dimension that was not addressed in the study is the impact a specific Philippine language may play in the type of self-repair strategies necessary for effective communication to take place among multilingual speakers in court proceedings. Self-repair in oral communication happens when speakers revise utterances in order to help listeners gain a better understanding of messages. In everyday conversations, speakers normally self-repair in their mother tongues. In situations where their mother tongue is a nondominant language, such as the case of courtroom hearings in English in the Philippines, how will self-repair happen? This dimension of language use was not tackled by Santos. Despite this, Santos's study is noteworthy in that it may represent the first attempt by a Filipino linguist to recognize in a formal study the multilingual context of legal proceedings in the country.

As previously mentioned, publications on FL as such began only in 2013 after the ISSFLA training in Malaysia in 2012. One of these studies is that of Martin (2013), which investigated court interpreting and the issues attached to the use of English as the language of the legal domain in the country. Like Santos's study in 2006, Martin underscored the vital role of interpreters in court hearings. In describing and analyzing court interpreting practices, Martin also identified the challenges Filipino interpreters face in the courtroom.

The English-centric language policy in the Philippines does not necessarily favor the majority of Filipinos who are not well versed in the language. It is in this context that Martin's work opens with a description of a noteworthy undertaking of the Supreme Court of the Philippines, through its Committee on Linguistic Concerns, which spearheaded the 2007 Bulacan Experiment aimed at promoting the use of Filipino in court proceedings, including stenographic notetaking. This project initially involved six Regional Trial Courts (RTCs) in Malolos, the capital city of the province of Bulacan, and one Municipal Trial Court (MTC) in the town of Guiguinto, also in Bulacan. Along the way, the RTCs and MTCs backed out, leaving only one regional trial court in Malolos to pursue the project under the supervision of Judge Ma.

Resurreccion Ramos-Buhat, who persisted with the use of Filipino in her court that was considered as a special court for drug cases. With her untimely demise, court hearings reverted to the use of English, which signaled the failure of the pilot project.

Martin's study demonstrates the challenges equally faced by court personnel. Her comparisons between official stenographic transcripts and audio recordings of hearings reveal that the notes prepared by court stenographers were inaccurate, despite the stenographers working closely with interpreters. In addition, when source utterances were back-translated by Martin to check the accuracy of the translations, it was found that court interpreters were unable to provide accurate translations. Untrained or lacking in court interpretation training, Filipino court interpreters truly struggle as they translate from English to Filipino. Indeed, the context of translation is complex as it involves legal language.

In the Philippines, court interpreters engage in other tasks aside from court interpretation. This is another concern raised by Martin. Aside from doing translation, court interpreters also mark exhibits introduced in evidence, prepare minutes of the court sessions, prepare court calendars, and record the cases scheduled for hearing. The Presiding Judge or the Branch Clerk of Court also concurrently assigns courtroom interpreters to perform other functions such that they also sometimes function as stenographers. Courtroom interpretation is no easy and simple task. With the addition of other expected functions, the quality of translation may be affected due to human limitations posed by workload fatigue in addition to a lack of proper linguistic training.

One can surmise that Martin's study evinces numerous issues that are relevant, but not fully discussed. The fact is that being in the courtroom is already a traumatic experience in itself for ordinary citizens; the use of English adds to the stressful situation, especially for the underprivileged. Martin's article, which pushes for the use of Filipino for those being interrogated, should serve as a starting point for the review of the language policy being implemented in the legal domain in the country. Indeed, much has to be done in terms of improving the delivery of justice in the Philippines and this has to start with a policy that proves beneficial not only to the judge and lawyers but also to the marginalized suspects and witnesses. Unless the policy is changed and stakeholders are convinced that the use of local languages simplifies courtroom proceedings and facilitates better communication among legal stakeholders, courtroom discourse including court interpreting will continue to be marked by uncertainty and doubt. Martin (2013, p. 9) aptly concludes with the following recommendation: "In multilingual contexts such as the Philippines, a system that accommodates languages other than English, such as a bilingual legal system where there is tolerance for switching from one language to another, should be seriously considered."

In a later study published in 2018, Martin made the same argument for using Filipino as the language of law in the Philippines, but also expanded on her 2013 proposal by calling for the inclusion of other Philippine languages. The Philippines, with around 185 local languages according to Ethnologue, is marked by great linguistic diversity. A disproportionate preference for Filipino as an additional language in court proceedings might only further relegate the other local languages to the background, which is a disservice to millions of Filipinos whose L1 is not Tagalog. Martin's arguments were supported by a survey conducted among lawyers and judges concerning the use of a dominant language at work and in courtroom tasks, as well as on the current language policy of using English in the courtroom, including the challenges encountered in using English at work. The results revealed that the dominant oral language spoken with colleagues at work is a Philippine language, but the dominant language for written tasks at work and for courtroom tasks is English. The results of the survey were corroborated by the results of the 2003/2004 Survey of Lawyers and Judges on the State of the Judiciary and the Legal Profession, which involved at least 400 lawyers and 889 judges, where a large percentage disagreed that Filipino or the local languages should be official in courts. The respondents further claimed that they rarely have a need for courtroom interpretation and have no difficulty in using English in the courtroom. Similarly, a large majority were content with the present language policy of Philippine courts, although a few expressed their difficulty in the litigation process when litigants are not familiar with English.

An argument that could be raised in this situation is that a similar survey should have been conducted to level the playing field. In the courtroom, it is evident that those who are interrogated, including suspects and witnesses, are typically the powerless. While all courtroom participants have a role to play, not everyone is given the same privilege to speak, which reveals the limitations in courtroom interactions. Simonett (1966 in Du, 2016) claims that the courtroom is similar to a stage where both contain drama, conflicting claims, a search for truth, the lure of money, love, and violence; these make for a great dramatic play. Given the relationship among the participants in the judicial proceedings, the institutional ideology of how justice is achieved in the Philippine courtroom is revealed.

One of the most prolific forensic linguists in the Philippines to date is Rañosa-Madrunio, who was also among the first to publish in 2013. Her first study on FL is an analysis of the questioning process in courtroom discourse, specifically focusing on the typology and structure of lawyers' questions, as well as the turn-taking practices in courtroom interrogation. In this study,

Rañosa-Madrunio argued that power asymmetry is enacted and legitimated in courtroom discourse involving lawyers (the interrogator) and suspects or witnesses (the interrogated).

The study opens with a recognition of the complexities of legal practice in multilingual contexts. In the Philippines, these complexities point to the prestige status of English, the official language of the courts, and how the language has become exclusionary. Rañosa-Madrunio's research study was set in one of the RTCs in Malolos, Bulacan, which conducted the well-documented Filipino-only experiment. The choice of research setting is commendable in that it allowed the study of courtroom discussions in both English (for civil cases) and Tagalog (for criminal cases involving drugs). However, the study would have been richer had it compared the enactment of power asymmetry between courtroom discourse in English and courtroom discourse in Tagalog. In addition, as power asymmetry is almost always expected between the interrogator and the interrogated, it would have been more beneficial to describe attempts at resisting power asymmetry, if any, in courtroom discourse.

Issues of power and control were later addressed by Rañosa-Madrunio in her 2014 study, which analyzed the pragmatics of direct and cross-examinations in a courtroom hearing corpus gathered from the same RTC in Malolos, Bulacan. This work is trailblazing in employing Critical Discourse Analysis (CDA) as a theoretical lens. It utilized an expansive set of tools in analyzing courtroom discourse; these included pragmatics, specifically the study of speech acts, politeness markers, silence, and face-threatening/saving acts. The study also went beyond linguistics by including the multimodal dimensions of gaze, facial expression, gesture, and postural orientation. Here, Rañosa-Madrunio looked into how group power relations are achieved and what social consequences emerge from these power relations. In terms of speech acts, questioning was found to be highly used. Politeness markers such as *po*, *ho*, *niyo*, and *kayo* were found in the Tagalog corpus. Silence was mostly used by witnesses, while lawyers employed face-threatening acts. A brief description of the multimodal conduct of courtroom personnel during hearings was also provided.

The analytic tools, though expansive, were not thoroughly and deeply utilized to fully expose power asymmetry in the courtroom. Similar to her 2013 work, this study did not attempt to compare the enactment of power asymmetry between the courtroom discourse in English and courtroom discourse in Tagalog, even though Rañosa-Madrunio concluded that "it would still be a better move to allow the witness to use a language s/he is most proficient in to prevent linguistic curtailment and to restrict the use of English especially with the disadvantaged lay to minimize the exercise of control" (Rañosa-Madrunio, 2014, p. 28).

Also focusing on the language of interrogation, Villanueva and Rañosa-Madrunio (2015) investigated the way lawyers cross-examined vulnerable and non-vulnerable witnesses in rape trials. The vulnerable witnesses in these cases were minors aged under eighteen at the time of the alleged rape and the study examined their court testimonials. The non-vulnerable witnesses in this study included doctors, teachers, suspects, and relatives of the victims who were older than eighteen and able to answer the lawyers' questions in court. The focus of the study was on the types of questions asked of both groups, the vulnerable and non-vulnerable witnesses, as well as on the kind of replies they gave.

Thirty-eight transcripts of stenographic notes (TSNs) from eight criminal cases were examined, consisting of 1,866 questions and 1,811 replies. All the criminal cases involved incestuous rape. Interesting findings were yielded by the study. In the case of vulnerable witnesses, the most common question types were in the form of tag, yes/no, *wh-*, and-tag, and so-tag questions. This finding is similar to that yielded for the non-vulnerable witnesses, where the most common question types were yes/no, *wh-*, and-yes, tag, and so-yes/no. It appears then that lawyers did not adjust their language when questioning the children and that there was no distinction in the questioning techniques used by the lawyers in investigating the young and the adults. It also appears that more forceful and coercive questions were asked of the vulnerable witnesses with the use of more tag questions. Regarding the categories for witnesses' answers, the response categories were in the form of compliance, resistance, giving and seeking clarification, misunderstanding, uncertainty, no response, and changes in the story/response.

Villanueva and Rañosa-Madrunio's study, as admitted by the authors, relied on TSNs, which are believed to be inaccurate representations of courtroom proceedings, as pointed out by Martin (2013) in her study of court interpreting comparing TSNs with the court's own audio recordings. In addition, the use of English in the litigation process, a language not readily understood by the witnesses, may have unduly affected stenographic notetaking. Fully aware of the limitations of their study, the authors conducted a semi-structured interview with the lawyers with regard to their predominant questioning styles and confirmed with the victims their types of replies. This was done in the hope of reducing the inaccuracy of the stenographic notes.

Noteworthy in the study is the attention to not only the linguistics of legal practice, but also to the non-linguistic aspects, specifically the physical setting of the courtroom. There should be a separate room for vulnerable witnesses so they are protected from their alleged assailants. When vulnerable witnesses, especially minors, become part of the interrogation process, their identities should be kept confidential by allowing them to wait in rooms that are separated from the courtrooms. Admittedly, lack of space is a problem in many Philippine courts and ample space cannot be assured for the conduct of delicate hearings, thus putting the identity of vulnerable people at stake. Safety of minors is jeopardized especially when they get into contact with their abusers inside the courtroom. In terms of physical setting, two striking concerns should be addressed in the Philippine justice system: (1) The inadequate facilities or poor physical conditions of the courtrooms and (2) safety problems. This does not discount the fact that in relation to the use of language, lawyers should also undergo more training in investigating child-related cases, most especially in their questioning techniques. The study judiciously touched on some of the pressing issues confronted by legal stakeholders in handling sensitive cases such as rape of minors.

A lawyer's role in legal interrogations is crucial. In the context of the Philippines and in many other countries as well, it is the judge who makes decisions on whether or not stories are true or untrue. Hence, a lawyer's ability to construct questions, as well as to counteract testimonies, will most certainly affect the witnesses' responses, and ultimately influence a judge's decision. Lawyers' questioning techniques, therefore, specifically the use of yes/no questions, may affirm and validate witnesses' claims or may also contradict what has been earlier stated by other witnesses.

Andrade and Ballesteros-Lintao, in a 2018 study, investigated questions asked by lawyers in court trials in an attempt to examine how control is exercised by Filipino lawyers. In particular, this study analyzed the use of yes/no questions in one case from an RTC that also functions as a special court for drug cases in the city of Manila. Since the study was interested in how control is exemplified in the lawyer's questioning techniques, the study focused on cross-examinations. This way, it could be seen how lawyers of one party aim to invalidate or contradict the version of the story constructed by the other party through direct examinations, thereby correspondingly creating their own version.

Despite the promising qualities of the study, the corpus used was limited to only one completed case with eight transcriptions, thus posing further limitations. For example, as Andrade and Ballesteros-Lintao themselves stressed, the findings could not serve as a basis for concluding how control is exercised by Filipino lawyers. The study may be seen as exploratory in nature where no robust conclusions are made. It is a good attempt at analyzing Philippine courtroom discourse, and could further be enhanced by looking into the degree of control practiced by legal professionals over lay participants to account for the uniqueness of the study in relation to other studies done in this area.

While the study of Andrade and Ballesteros-Lintao focused on questioning in court proceedings, a corpus study by Del Rosario and Ballesteros-Lintao (2018) analyzed the investigative interviewing practices of law enforcement authorities in two cities in Metro Manila. The corpus consisted of fifteen transcripts of audio-recorded interviews of police officers investigating adolescents involved in crime against property. From these transcripts, 944 questions were coded following Shepherd's (2007) conversation management approach and Gibbons' four-phased Cognitive Interview (2003) framework. Shepherd's framework includes three categories to classify the forms of questioning: (1) Productive questioning, which is a non-coercive approach to obtaining initial information from a suspected offender using the five *wh*-questions; (2) risky questioning or polar interrogatives/tag questions, which include forms such as closed yes/no questions and open confirmatory questions that commence with *could you/if/ whether*; and (3) counter-productive questioning, which are confirmation-seeking questions considered to be the most coercive of all the categories. Gibbons' (2003) framework, meanwhile was used to explore discourse structures employed by the police, and looks into the following phases in Cognitive Interviewing: (1) Rapport building phase where the interviewee is made to relax and reduce the trauma of the initial interview by way of discussing topics unrelated to the case to earn their trust; (2) free narrative phase or free recall where a narrative of events is elicited using the interviewee's own words; (3) questioning phase where the interviewer confirms the details of the crime committed using lower and higher-order thinking question types; and (4) closure phase where investigative officers summarize the account and secure information from the alleged offenders and recycle the questioning stage as a debriefing strategy.

Employing the framework of Shepherd (2007), the findings revealed that with the 944 coded questions, the following question types were employed in this order: counter-productive, productive, and risky. Counter-productive questions limit the opportunity for the alleged youth offenders to produce narrative responses and to elaborate further on the information they just provided. It was also found that coercive and intimidating techniques in the questioning process did not actually lead to obtaining sufficient information needed in the case. Using Gibbons' (2003) framework, the results revealed that the questioning phase had the greatest number of occurrences. In fact, out of the 944 utterances, 467 were categorized under the questioning phase. However, Del Rosario and Ballesteros-Lintao (2018) also noted that the Filipino police interviewers failed to follow a specific structure during the interview process and that some questions raised were not aligned to the Cognitive Interview structure. A mismatch therefore was identified between the questioning strategies and the goals for the interview process. With these findings, Del Rosario and Ballesteros-Lintao then recommended that further training of the cognitive interviewing skills of police interviewers be carried out and that a review of existing guidelines for interviewing children in conflict with the law (CICL) be initiated to achieve improved results from the interviews of alleged youth offenders. This can be attained by way of establishing rapport with the offenders, which also takes into consideration their psychological welfare.

It is noted that the authors' use of conversational analysis and Jefferson's system of transcription failed to include the finer details of the complete conversations that took place between interviewers and interviewees. Thus, the complex nature of interaction between the interviewer and the interviewee was not captured in detail. The authors could have shown the strengths and weaknesses of police investigative interviewing in order to pave the way for the further improvement of interview methods involving youth offenders. Still, it should be acknowledged that the study of Del Rosario and Ballesteros-Lintao is one of a handful to engage in investigative interviewing of police officers, which is difficult to do in the Philippines. The authors' efforts are thus commendable.

Picking up from earlier studies on court interpreting, Martin (2013) among them, Jimenez and Ballesteros-Lintao (2020) conducted a norm-based analysis of court interpretation in criminal cases in the Philippines. A major challenge in embarking on such a study is the absence of norms and regulations for court interpreting in the Philippines. Unlike court interpreting elsewhere in the world, the practice in the Philippines is not approached as a professional discipline, and does not seem to be taken seriously by legal stakeholders. The researchers therefore had to look to Australia, the United States, and Europe to formulate a research framework for the study. Jimenez and Ballesteros-Lintao's study is thus anchored on the Code of Ethics for court interpreters developed by the Australian Institute of Interpreters and Translators (AUSIT), the European Association for Legal Interpreters and Translators (EULITA), and the US-based National Association of Judiciary Interpreters and Translators (NAJIT), Inc.

The corpus consisted of eleven audio recordings of court proceedings that were transcribed and analyzed to determine adherence to the six norms of accuracy, impartiality, competence, professional conduct, and professional relationships. The authors found that the norm of accuracy had the highest occurrence at 120 instances, followed by the norms of impartiality and compe-tence. The norm of confidentiality was not found in the corpus. This was attributed to the fact that the norm of confidentiality could not be identified by simply analyzing the exchange of utterances alone. In the end, Jimenez and

Ballesteros-Lintao conclude that there is substantial evidence of adherence to all the six norms in the corpus. They add that accuracy ranks high in the list of norms and that "the interpreters strive to achieve accuracy by putting together their cultural knowledge as well as their proficiency in both English and Filipino" (Jimenez & Ballesteros-Lintao, 2020, p. 150).

The dominance of the English language in Philippine courtroom hearings renders court interpreting necessary in Philippine legal practice. However, this also calls attention to the need to strengthen court interpreting practices to ensure just and fair court proceedings. As has been demonstrated in earlier studies (such as Martin, 2013), court interpreting was not seen to be a serious professional discipline in the Philippines. Thus this study of Jimenez and Ballesteros-Lintao significantly contributes to a growing body of research on court interpreting in the country. It calls for the monitoring and regulating of court interpretation practices for the benefit of those who are not proficient in the dominant language of the courts.

Deuna and Ballesteros-Lintao (2022) made use of the Appraisal Framework, which is associated with Michael Halliday's Systemic Functional Linguistics or SFL (Martin 2000; Martin & White 2005), to analyze the language of evaluation in criminal cases involving drugs. In particular, the study examined the attitudinal resources used by court participants in the use of evaluative language in courtroom discourse. The Appraisal Framework comprises the three systems of Attitude, Engagement, and Gradation, with each having its own subsystems. This study focuses only on the system of *Attitude*, which is concerned with the functions of *Affect*, *Judgment*, and *Appreciation*.

The corpus consisted of official court transcripts of one criminal case in an RTC in Manila, a special court for drug cases. This case had twenty-three official transcripts, which were analyzed to identify items of *Attitude* and their frequency and usage. The results revealed the following: (1) Attitude expressing is a function of legal terms; (2) evaluation is mostly implicitly expressed; and (3) there is awareness among the lawyers of the role they play as officers of the court. In addition, the *Attitude* subcategory of *Judgment* was found to be the most prevalent valuation, with Tenacity as the most evident appraisal subcategory. The Attitude category of Appreciation was moderately expressed. The least prevalent among the Attitude categories was Affect, which is expected in courtroom proceedings that tend to avoid personal and emotional expressions.

Despite its complexity, SFL is an effective theoretical tool in raising awareness of language choices and of the impact of such choices on the communicative event. Deuna and Ballesteros-Lintao (2002, p. 191) assert that "the study presented the potentiality of the language of evaluation in courtroom discourse and posited that the language in the court is also influenced by human factors such that evaluations and attitude expressing is also a characteristic of court-room discourse." However, it would have been more beneficial to stakeholders if the authors had made some effort to account for the unique context of drug cases in the study. In 2021, it was reported that there were almost 42,000 drug cases in the country, with a significantly large number found in the provinces of Cavite, Laguna, Batangas, Rizal, and Quezon (Region 4-A) (Statista, 2022). Former Philippine President Rodrigo Duterte waged a violent drug war that cost the lives of many Filipinos. The issue of illegal drugs is of utmost interest to many, including the Catholic Church, which sees the problem as very much related to poverty. Thus, any study on illegal drugs would contribute significantly to understanding the problem, as well as resolving it.

The studies reviewed above represent research that focused mainly on language in legal processes, including courtroom discourse and investigative interviewing. They are in fact the most commonly used corpora in FL studies in the country. In the Philippines, gathering such corpora poses various challenges. In many instances, one has to do much networking in the legal sector to acquire relevant data. The problems cited in these studies are quite serious too. For example, the courtroom interpreters' lack of language training imposes great complications to the development of cases, including the proper practice of legal procedures and ensuring the veracity of information for ordinary people who are not proficient in English. With English likewise as the primary medium in courtroom questioning processes, no assurance can be made that fair and just proceedings would be carried out given that the interrogated typically do not have full command of the language. This practice extends to the investigative interviewing of law enforcement authorities. How then will the disadvantaged respond confidently and accurately if they can barely understand what they are being asked?

Indeed, the prestigious status of English in the country is only for the privileged few who have better access to education and other resources. Thus, a serious review of the language policy as it is applied to the legal domains must be undertaken. This should include written legal documents that seem difficult to understand due to the use of legalese. Added to this concern is the physical structure of courtrooms in the Philippines, which are often restricted by a lack of adequate space to keep minors safe, especially during hearings of sensitive cases. As pointed in the earlier part of this section, the studies on courtroom discourse and investigative interviewing have also exposed the weaknesses of legal practice in the Philippines.

The next set of studies illustrates how the language of legal texts, in addition to legal practices, has tended to push Filipinos further to the margins. It is important to note how legal language makes a legal text incomprehensible to ordinary readers. One can easily underscore the gap that exists between legal language and ordinary language. With the various linguistic features of legal language that set it apart from a layperson's language, including the use of foreign words from Latin and French, archaisms, embedded structures, nominalizations, and passives among others, legal language is far from being easily accessible to nonlawyers or by those outside the legal profession.

One of the earlier studies on the language of the law is that of Gocheco (2007), who conducted a genre-based analysis of legal provisions in the Philippine real estate industry. The corpus, which consisted of fourteen legal provisions on property ownership and other real estate laws from the Philippine Civil Code, was subjected to an analysis of lexico-grammatical features and cognitive structures. The study attempted to explain the complexity and peculiarity of legal language. This exhaustive analysis of the lexico-grammatical features of legal provisions in the Civil Code is noteworthy in Gocheco's research, considering that this study was one of the first few attempts at FL analysis in the country. Gocheco presented the following findings:

1. In terms of sentence length, the average number was 51.4 words, with the longest sentence made up of 272 words.
2. For nominal structure, an average of 16.8 nominal structures were found in the sentences, with a significant number of repetitions, and almost no use of pronouns and similar references.
3. The sentences were not found to contain complex prepositional phrases, which the author found "surprising" (Gocheco, 2007, p. 113).
4. There was a high occurrence of syntactic discontinuities, a total of eighty-five occurrences with an average of 6.07 insertions per sentence.
5. In terms of cognitive structuring, a two-part move structure (Provisional Clause and Qualifications) was found to characterize the legal provisions.

As in other early studies on the interface between language and the law, Gocheco aimed to connect findings to the training of ESP teachers and learners, particularly for the teaching of English to those interested in engaging the real estate industry. The study aimed to "provide a simplified description of legal provisions that can be used in ESP training" (Gocheco, 2007, p. 101). However, apart from knowledge about the features of legal language, it is not clear how the findings of the study may directly impact English-language learning, or how knowledge about the language of laws on real estate properties may benefit stakeholders.

The study of Marasigan and Ballesteros-Lintao (2020) on the comprehensibility of public policies takes on a more inclusive, user-oriented position by focusing on how the language of the law may become more accessible to the ordinary Filipino. In their study, Marasigan and Ballesteros-Lintao sought to address how public policies are presented in online news articles and how readers comprehend them. Forty online articles were collected from January to December 2017 through the websites of two leading broadsheet newspapers in the Philippines, namely, the *Manila Bulletin* and the *Philippine Daily Inquirer*. The laws subjected to analysis were Republic Act No. 10931 or the Universal Access to Quality Tertiary Education Act (also known as the Free Tuition Law) and Republic Act 10963 or the Tax Reform for Acceleration and Inclusion (TRAIN). Using Pan and Kosicki's (1993) Framing Analysis, the study determined how laws were incorporated in the news articles by analyzing the articles' syntactic structure. Marasigan and Ballesteros-Lintao sought to determine the placement or location of the laws in the news articles through applying the inverted pyramid structure, which is the main component of the syntactic structure of framing proposed by Pan and Kosicki (1993). This inverted pyramid structure deals with the sequential organization of structural elements of new reports. It has four parts: (1) The lead described as the "key" to the story that summarizes the five Ws and H of the account; (2) secondary information which is an extension of the five Ws and H; (3) background information which includes the incidents that lead to or follow the event; and (4) additional information which adds details of the story. The paragraphs containing any information about the public policies were likewise classified according to the following presentation styles: (1) Direct reference, (2) indirect reference, (3) description, (4) effect, (5) objective, and (6) comparison. Finally, the study determined the comprehensibility of the texts for the lay readers in relation to how the details of the laws are embedded in these texts. A focus group discussion (FGD) was conducted with five randomly sampled articles from each law used as reference for discussion. Through this FGD, the per-ceived ease or difficulty in understanding specific public policies as presented in online news articles was determined.

The findings revealed that most of the articles analyzed fall under the category of secondary information. Furthermore, the study also showed that public policy related news articles had similar dominant presentation styles, specifically, directly referencing the name of the law and indicating its specific provisions. As regards comprehensibility, the majority of the articles were not found to be easily comprehended by the readers since most of the news articles focused more on the events and issues surrounding the policy, rather than the provisions of the law itself. Added to this was the fact that the articles included terms not easily understood by the readers because of their complexity and formality.

Marasigan and Ballesteros-Lintao's study highlighted the importance of accurately presenting public policies in new articles. Because these policies are crafted in response to social issues, it may take years before a public policy is put into place. It would be a waste if all the efforts of the government in formulating public policies do not reach the ordinary people simply because the presentation styles of news articles are problematic and the message is unclear. A key takeaway from this study is the value of examining the presentation of public policies in news articles, whether in print or online, using the Framing Analysis Framework. Presentation styles and text comprehensibility should also be investigated by way of testing readers' understanding of the provisions of the law, as presented in news articles. Only then can one say that these public policies are truly relevant as they have been crafted for the ordinary citizen.

Unlike the journal articles discussed in this Elements section, the work of Garcia-Jawid is a book published in 2009. It is among the first few early publications on FL in the Philippines. Inspired by the fact that most studies done on legal language and legal decisions of courts primarily focused on lexico-grammatical features and macrostructure patterns of discourse types, this book looks into how Philippine culture and its strong patriarchal orientation are enmeshed in the court decisions by selected RTCs in Las Pinas City, Metro Manila. Garcia-Jawid attempts to reveal power structures that favor one gender group over the other. The book likewise investigates the extra-textual features that affect the way meanings from these are negotiated.

With the goal of identifying and explaining the range of sociocultural perspectives present in legal decisions, such as patriarchal tenor, indirectness, and ambiguity, Garcia-Jawid subjected twenty sample cases to rigorous linguistic and discourse analysis. Patriarchal tenor is manifested in the way generic pronouns are understood with the use of *he*, which is sex specific and associated with a strong male image, thus promoting the view that the world is male dominated. Moreover, the analysis revealed instances of patriarchal tenor based on identified categories such as misuse of generic pronouns, the marking of women, and sexist language. Indirectness was exemplified through the use of nominalizations and passive verb forms, while ambiguity was made apparent through the use of indirect expression and euphemism. Word sense (e.g. improper or awkward word choice or usage), structural (e.g. problematic syntax and sentence construction), and referential (e.g. unclear antecedents) categories of ambiguity were included. Considering that ambiguity was given preference in the discussion, this could have paved the way for the author to address a pressing issue relating to the language used in legal documents. While legal documents are written primarily for legal professionals, there are instances when these documents are prepared for non-legal professionals. Thus, pushing for the use of plain language to make legal documents readily comprehensible to the ordinary citizen is a timely and relevant matter to be discussed and given preferential attention.

While this concern on the use of plain language is already advanced in countries such as the UK, the United States, and Canada, much has to be done with regard to promoting this movement in the Philippines. Senator Grace Poe, who was then the head of the Senate Committee on Public Information in the country in 2013, passed Senate Bill No. 1092 known as "An Act Enhancing Citizens' Access to Government Information and Services by Requiring All Government Documents to be Written in Plain Language and if Necessary, Translated to Local Language or Dialect." This was patterned after the Public Law 111–274 enacted by the US Congress in 2010 intended "to improve the effectiveness and accountability of Federal agencies to the public" by promoting government communication that the public can understand and use.

The Plain Language Movement shares the goal of successful communication. The intention is to avoid the use of jargon, ambiguity, and obscurity. Section Three of the bill highlights that all government agencies in the country should adopt plain writing in all their communications and in the implementation of their basic functions, mandates, and services. It likewise provides that plain writing be used in, but not limited to, information about any government benefit or service; forms necessary for obtaining any government benefit or filing taxes; and documents that explain to the public how to comply with a requirement the government agencies seek to administer, enforce, and provide. In other words, according to the bill, plain writing shall also cover letters, forms, instructions, notices, and publications, and all government agencies, including state-run corporations, will be required to adopt plain writing on their websites or relevant portals. The aim, therefore, is to help citizens in accessing government services. To date, there has still been very little progress in terms of its implementation by Philippine authorities.

While Garcia-Jawid analyzed RTC decisions, Hernandez (2017) and Balgos (2017), in two separate studies, worked on the language of Supreme Court decisions. For Hernandez, the focus was on a stylistic analysis of adverbials of attitude and emphasis in Philippine English. The corpus consisted of fifty-four decisions on civil cases crafted by two Filipino Supreme Court chief justices. Hernandez investigated the placement of adverbials in these documents, as well as their contexts in a sentence. As in other previous studies that linked the language of legal texts to ESP, this study likewise attempted to draw implications of the findings for the teaching of English for Legal Purposes (ELP). While ELP as a field exists in the Philippines, it is seldom talked about and researched on. In fact, only a few studies can be identified that address the challenges of law school education and determine the implications for legal English pedagogy. In other words, English-language specialists and legal professionals work together to address the needs of academia and legal practice.

It is worth noting that this study employed data not often used in legal discourse studies. Supreme Court decisions are prepared by different justices or lawyers and, therefore, reflect various writing styles. This is not to discount the fact that they may be guided by certain standards in crafting judgments. While there are those that are lengthy, as in the case of permanent injunctions, contract performance, and document cancellations, there are also short decisions, such as reviews, preliminary issues, and summary suits. Each corpus set contained at least 1,000–5,000 words, totaling 160,087 words. In analyzing the corpus, the frameworks of Finegan (2012), Quirk and colleagues (1985), and Dita (2011) were employed. The adverbials were examined based on the following categories and subcategories: *Adverbials of attitude*, which were further classified into (a) evaluation of the subject of the clause, and (b) judgment of the whole clause; *adverbials of emphasis*, which were further classified into (a) conviction and (b) doubt. With regard to *adverbials of location*, they were categorized into (a) initial, (b) medial, and (c) final. Finally, as regards environment in sentences, they were categorized into their collocation (a) in split infinitives, (b) with functors or function words, (c) before conjunctions, and (d) within a noun phrase.

Interesting findings were yielded by the study. For instance, in relation to the categories of these adverbials, the two justices employed evaluation of the subject of the clause and judgment of the whole clause under adverbials of attitude but a third classification emerged, which was evaluation of an action performed by the subject of the clause. For adverbials of emphasis, commonly employed were those of conviction and doubt. In addition, while differences were noted in the placement of adverbials in sentences, one dominant feature surfaced, which was the placement of adverbials in the medial position. Another fascinating result in the study is the discovery that while the adverbials have four environments in a sentence such as in a split infinitive, with functor or function word, before a conjunction, and within a noun phrase, three other categories were identified. These were (a) before/after the verb, (b) after an intensifier, and (c) *not applicable* (N/A), referring to adverbials in the initial position which evaluate the whole clause, and which appear before the subject of the sentence. According to the author, N/A was used to avoid confusion stemming from the classes of adverbials of attitude and emphasis.

As an implication for the teaching of ELP, the study recommends that the teaching of adverbials of attitude and emphasis in the ELP classroom be prioritized, taking into consideration the classifications, placements, and environments of these adverbials. Since the language used in the corpus was taken from select decisions of two Supreme Court justices, the Philippine variety of English was used in the documents. These two adverbials in Supreme Court decisions expose students in the legal domain to the variety of English used, which is Philippine English, as well as to the style of writing Supreme Court decisions.

Balgos's study (2017) on argumentation in Philippine and American Supreme Court decisions is an interesting study of two areas in linguistics: the use of varieties of English in legal discourse and argumentation in the legal genre. While numerous studies have been conducted on the varieties of English, particularly Philippine English versus American English, this study provides a fresh flavor in that Supreme Court decisions served as the data for analysis. The specificity of the investigation, which focused on the distinct instances of concessions, is worth noting as it tried to establish the connection between judicial argumentation theory and linguistics by closely examining the concessive patterns and how they contribute to the realization of concession. This stage of analysis involved doing a thorough manual count of the concessive devices used in Move 5 (Arguing the case) from all the data, which include: (1) concessive conjunctions, (2) concessive disjuncts, (3) concessive verbs, (4) attitudinal disjuncts, (5) conditional conjunctions, (6) modals of possibility, and (7) truth-evaluation phrases. However, no inter-coding was employed. Considering that legal language employs a complex syntax and structure, the concessive moves examined included fragmented and full sentences and whole paragraphs.

Interestingly, the results of the study showed that Philippine Supreme Court decisions scored higher in terms of concessive signals than the American Supreme Court decisions, revealing that the Filipino judges employed more concessive patterns in asserting judicial decisions than American judges. These concessive signals are (1) *however*, the most frequently used concessive disjunct; and (2) *although*, the most preferred concessive conjunction. Whereas the former needed more concessive devices signaling multiple concessions in a single decision, the latter enunciated decisions in the simplest way possible.

Judging from the findings, the article appears to set the direction for analyzing the current trends in the language of jurisprudence. As the interactional model of concessions may be applied in analyzing judicial jurisprudence, it was inferred from the study that both Philippine and American Supreme Court decisions are similar in terms of employing the Pseudo-Dyadic Concessive Schema, perhaps due to the fact that the Court wants to guarantee that all claims of the lower courts have been reviewed and acknowledged before the verdict for the case is released. According to Balgos (2017), in the Pseudo-Dyadic Schema, the concessive pattern is initiated by one participant who takes an opposing view, acknowledges the preceding claim, and produces a counterclaim that downgrades the conceded proposition. This is an added feature of the article in that after analyzing the linguistic feature of concession in both varieties, a contrastive analysis was done revealing that native speakers of English utilize a wider array of concessive signals when writing jurisprudential decisions.

Considering that the study employed thorough manual counting of concessives, a computational analysis could provide richer results. With the use of concordancer tools such as *Antconc*, there may be less likelihood of some tokens being inadvertently left out, which may possibly happen. It follows then that there will be more insights that can be gleaned from the results, including collocations of words in the concessions identified. Since the study examined various types of concessions such as concessive conjunctions, concessive disjuncts, concessive verbs, attitudinal disjuncts, conditional conjunctions, modals of possibility, and truth-evaluation phrases, these search words along with the collocates and the listing of these words based on frequency could lead to richer insights or discussions. The use of manual analysis may also serve as a reason for the employment of inter-coding so that a validation could have been done for the initial results yielded.

From RTC decisions to Supreme Court decisions, Filipino forensic linguists have also studied decisions made in international courts of law, such as the Arbitral Tribunal, which heard the case of the Philippines against China in the South China Sea Territorial dispute. In their study, Madrilejos and Ballesteros-Lintao (2020) examined the interpretation process of the Arbitral Tribunal in the judgment of the South China Sea conflict between China and the Philippines. The goal of the study was to reconstruct and investigate the interpretation of written arguments made by the concerned parties. The study takes a relevance-theoretic perspective focusing on the logical condition, the pragmatic condition, and the condition of optimal relevance on the Permanent Court of Arbitration's decision on the South China Sea territorial dispute. From this perspective, the researchers argue that valid interpretations of the written documents of both parties were made by the Arbitral Tribunal.

The choice of corpus, as well as the context of use of the written documents, are noteworthy in that the researchers recognize the importance of the interpretation of these documents to Philippine territorial rights. The study draws attention to an urgent international issue concerning Chinese encroachment on Philippine seas. In addition, there are very few, if any, studies on arbitration discourse that concern Philippine cases. In this regard, the study contributes to paving a path for scholars of language and law studies in the country. By employing Relevance Theory, they were able to present the logic of the decisions of the Arbitral Tribunal, thus underscoring the lack of merit of China's objections to the decisions.

This critical review of the studies done on language and law reveals that even though FL as a young field of study was formally introduced to the country less than a decade ago, the choice of data has taken on a new "face." In language and law studies, most deal with Supreme Court decisions, Miranda rights, and courtroom proceedings such as trial discourse and prosecution and defense closing speeches, to name a few. While there were studies done along that line reviewed herein, the choice of corpora revealed a preference for data considered not commonplace such as legal provisions in the real estate industry, Republic Acts, Philippine culture in court decisions by RTCs, comparison of select Philippine and American Supreme Court decisions, use of Philippine English in Supreme Court decisions, and the interpretation process of the Arbitral Tribunal in relation to the South China Sea conflict between China and the Philippines. This means that the topics selected by Filipino researchers and emerging scholars tread a new path, pioneering some areas in FL research which are of great use in the context of the Philippines.

The studies that follow also focus on the language of legal texts and are concerned with legal contracts, product warnings, and patient information materials. Ballesteros-Lintao and Rañosa-Madrunio have conducted three studies that analyze consumer finance contracts. The first of these, published in 2014, investigated a consumer finance contract for a credit card facility of a leading Philippine bank. The goal was to determine the contract's level of comprehensibility to its target readers. The contract contains 28 provisions, 51 paragraphs, 125 sentences, and 5,497 words. This study draws on a previous unpublished study of the authors in which they made use of a cloze test and paraphrasing test to determine the readability of the same consumer finance contract. It was concluded that Filipino readers of the contract have reading levels that range from those of Grades 6 to 8 students. The consumer finance contract was then compared to Cutts's (2011) Plain English Lexicon, revealing a significant number of words in the contract that may be considered as incomprehensible to its readers. The lexical analysis of the contract generated 120 words, 33 of which were Level 6 words, and at least 5 were Level 13 words in Cutts's guide. It was inferred from a close scrutiny of the words that regardless of lexical level, readers of such consumer contracts are unfamiliar with some words. These include the words *intention* (Level 6), *undertaking* (Level 8), *herein* (Level 10), *constitute* (Level 12), *incurred* (Level 12), and *terminate* (Level 12). In addition, the contract generated a number of words considered "unusually used" (Ballesteros-Lintao and Rañosa-Madrunio, 2014, p. 366), thereby adding to the complexity of the text and lowering the comprehensibility of the contract.

Several investigations have already pointed to the inaccessibility of consumer finance contracts (Schuck, 1992; Tiersma, 1999; Campbell, 2003; Gibbons, 2004; Bhatia, 2010; Williams, 2011), while others have called for the use of Plain English in such documents (Felsenfeld & Siegel, 1981; Tiersma, 1999; Eagleson, 2004). Unfortunately, these studies only apply to non-Philippine contexts, thus making the 2014 study by Ballesteros-Lintao and Rañosa-Madrunio on the lexical properties of a consumer finance contract a pioneering work in the field of Philippine FL. In addition, their study supports the call for the use of more comprehensible, reader-friendly contracts that is advocated by the Plain English Movement.

The study offers a lexical analysis of a consumer finance contract using the categories in Cutts's inventory of English lexicon. Although the study is pioneering in the Philippine context, it does not account for the fact that the language of choice of Philippine contracts is English, a de facto language of commerce yet quite foreign to many Filipinos. Thus, Cutts's inventory and categories, which are based on native speaker contexts (American and British), may not completely explain the complexity and unintelligibility of contracts to Filipino consumers. This may be the reason why the study found that even Level 6 words are unfamiliar to the readers of the contract. Further, the contract itself may have been modeled after American credit card contracts; thus by its very nature, the linguistic conventions of the contract may not match the sociolinguistic profile of its Philippine readers.

Ballesteros-Lintao and Rañosa-Madrunio, in 2015, further highlight the pressing concerns of credit card users in their financial transactions with banks. This study brought to the attention of consumers the importance of comprehending credit contract provisions. Since the 1980s, many had applied for credit cards, but few were aware of the fact that credit card terms and conditions (CCTCs) are classified as contracts of adhesion in which consumers do not have the right to reach a deal with the other party. As CCTCs are printed in bulk, these do not require formal agreements between parties; there is no clause-by-clause bargaining on either side, and only one party (the consumer) adheres to the terms of the contract, hence the label *contract of adhesion*. Many consumers do not carefully and thoroughly read contracts, and thus no full understanding of provisions takes place. In fact, with the small font size of the letters in CCTCs, not many consumers will bother to read the entire contract before signing it. The provision which states the compounding interest becomes clearer only as the consumer receives the statement of account on a monthly basis and sees the credit charges due. Aggravating this problem is the fact that the language used in CCTCs is legal in nature and so beyond the comprehension of the ordinary consumer.

It is worth mentioning that Ballesteros-Lintao and Rañosa-Madrunio (2015) employed a robust method in assessing the comprehensibility of one CCTC. The study employed the framework of Gibbons' (2012) Communication Evidence (Decision Trees) to find out whether there was meaning transfer from the text to a select group of thirty-five respondents. These respondents were also asked to take part in two reader-based tests (cloze and paraphrase) to determine the comprehensibility of the contract, which were supplemented by responses to open- and close-ended questions in which respondents wrote down their views about the comprehensibility of and familiarity with the document. It is alarming to note that almost 75 percent of the participants found the document to be largely incomprehensible. The respondents' perceived lack of understanding and familiarity was found to have a statistically significant relationship with their low paraphrase test scores. This finding was compounded by the results of questions asked of the participants, which revealed their difficulty in understanding the complex concepts and the difficult subject matter as well as complaints about the intricacies of the texts.

With these results, indeed, the use of Plain English in legal documents such as CCTCs should be further and actively promoted in the country. So far, even with the initiatives undertaken by the Philippine Congress in the past ten years and Senate Bill 1092, patterned after the US Plain Writing Act of 2010, a significant change on how contracts are prepared is yet to be realized.

Ballesteros-Lintao and Rañosa-Madrunio take their advocacy for the use of Plain English in legal texts to the next level in their 2017 work that takes a holistic and user-centered design approach in simplifying CCTCs. The goal of simplification is to ensure the usability and comprehensibility of the CTCCs at the first encounter of the document. The corpus of the study was a one-page document with 28 provisions and stipulations, 51 paragraphs, 125 sentences, and 5,497 words. The process for simplification that was employed in the study consisted of initial testing and three cycles of protocol-aided revision. For the initial testing phase, the corpus was analyzed for lexical (the presence of legalese) and syntactic (long and complex sentences) challenges and revised to eliminate the challenges. After this phase, protocol-aided revisions commenced in which fifteen participants were asked to read aloud the CTCC, paraphrase it, and formulate a version of the CTCC that is more usable and comprehensible to them. The result is a CTCC that is simple and user-driven.

What is noteworthy in this study by Ballesteros-Lintao and Rañosa-Madrunio is the recognition of the linguistic repertoire of the users of the CTCC; the researchers allowed the participants to speak in any language of their choice, in this case, English, Tagalog, and a mix of these languages. In addition, the user-centered framework itself is already a strength, especially in that the goal of the study is a simplified version of the CTCC without sacrificing the original content of the document. It is noted though that it would have been more beneficial if the process for protocol-aided revisions had been detailed enough for readers to benefit from a study that is anchored on a user-centered framework.

Other than consumer finance contracts, another form of legal text subjected to linguistic analysis is the memorandum of agreement (MOA), a common legal contract made between two collaborating parties, such as higher education institutions. Rañosa-Madrunio's (2020) study on the legal value of MOAs in academic partnerships is a descriptive and analytical study that replicates Alido's (2019) method of analysis of move structures. The corpus of Rañosa-Madrunio's research consisted of twenty MOAs between local and international academic institutions. Of these twenty MOAs, ten involved partnerships between local Philippine universities, while the other ten involved partnerships between Philippine universities and foreign universities. In analyzing the MOAs, the researcher was guided by the elements of legal contracts, which include (1) offer and acceptance; (2) mutual consent; (3) consideration; (4) competence; (5) legal purpose; and (6) written instrument. The MOAs also made use of the requisites identified in the Philippine Civil Code for contracts, which are (1) subject; (2) content; and (3) obligations. The study found that regardless of the nature of the collaboration between the two parties, whether between local universities or with a foreign university partner, the same moves were employed in the MOAs. It was also found that except for one, the MOAs did not have an Operative Part (which includes a Definition of Terms) and an Arbitration Clause, which may create legal issues in cases where one party does not fulfill its part of the MOA.

With the rapid increase of internationalization projects in Philippine universities, there is also an increased demand for MOAs between collaborating educational institutions. These MOAs, although considered legally as a contract, tend to be ill-prepared, short, formulaic, and not taken seriously. Thus, the choice of MOAs as the corpus of this study and, more importantly, foregrounding these as legally binding documents for academic collaboration among universities is noteworthy.

In another study on MOAs in academic partnerships, Rañosa-Madrunio in 2022 analyzed the corpus in her earlier work, but this time subjected the texts to a linguistic analysis using Johnson and Coulthard's (2010) framework for analyzing the linguistic features of legal documents. The lexical and grammatical features of the MOAs were analyzed, focusing specifically on (a) binomial expressions, (b) complex prepositions, (c) generic/cognitive structuring, (d) impersonal noun phrase constructions, (e) legal archaisms, (f) modality,

(g) negation, (h) nominalization, (i) passive constructions, (j) sentence length and complexity, and (k) specialized, distinctive, and technical legal lexis. From the analysis, the conclusion made by Rañosa-Madrunio is that the MOAs, just like any contract, are characterized by linguistic features that are intended for specific functions such as formalizing an agreement between two parties and ensuring that a safety net is provided to institutions that enter into an agreement without compromising their policies.

Another set of very interesting legal texts analyzed by forensic linguists in the country are product warnings. Dacumos and Rañosa-Madrunio (2015) analyzed the lexical features of product warnings in order to determine the comprehensibility of the texts and, ultimately, ensure the safety of consumers. This study is pioneering and significant in drawing attention to the importance of household chemical product warnings in ensuring both the safety of consumers and the protection of manufacturers from legal liabilities. The importance of product warnings, especially of potentially hazardous consumer products, cannot be underestimated. Product warnings are expected to protect consumers, while at the same time providing legal protection for manufacturers. The corpus of this work was a set of fifty product warnings on the usage and storage of household chemicals typically consumed by female household members (home makers and household helpers) in the Philippines. The household chemicals included laundry detergents, dishwashing liquids, fabric conditioners, toilet bowl cleaners, insect killers, air fresheners, solvents, and paint. The study employed frequency count in investigating five lexical categories, namely, nouns, words in field continuum (everyday vs. specialized words), signal words, adjectives, and adverbs. The findings included the following:

- As regards nouns, concrete nouns were found in 28 percent of the corpus, while abstract nouns were found in 44 percent, and nouns that point to unobservable phenomena were found in 16 percent of the corpus.
- In the case of word choice, everyday words made up 68 percent of the corpus, while specialized vocabulary made up 48 percent. Twelve percent of the product warnings contained highly technical words.
- All the product warnings contained signal words that indicate the degree of danger posed by the products, with the word "caution" the most frequently used.
- For adjectives, "harmful" was found in 30 percent of the product warnings, while "fatal" was found in 8 percent of the corpus.
- Thirty-six percent of the product warnings made use of adverbs in the postverbal position, while 28 percent made use of temporal adverbs.

These findings present product warnings as artifacts of an imagined "bond which connects the product manufacturers to product consumers" (Dacumos & Rañosa-Madrunio, 2015, p. 6). Product warnings are presented as modes through which manufacturers may directly communicate to consumers. However, the artifacts only offer a one-way communication mode that may be biased in favor of the interest of the manufacturers. Perhaps the concern of the study is geared towards the protection of consumers from incomprehensible product warnings. Additionally, the study is silent about language choice, specifically on the fact that the product warnings are largely in English, similar to CCTCs, which is not necessarily the first language of the target consumers of the household chemicals. From the corpus, there is mention of the use of the Tagalog term *babala* 'caution' in a product warning. A future study focusing on the use of Tagalog in product warnings and the implications of using Tagalog in the comprehensibility of the text will be of interest to ordinary Filipino consumers.

From household chemicals, Dacumos and Rañosa-Madrunio (2017) move to beauty products, which are also directed to female consumers. This study of the lexico-syntactic features of beauty product warnings begins with the premise that "consumers remain susceptible to a certain degree of risks associated with beauty-product use," despite efforts of manufacturers to be "vigilant and watchful" in crafting product warnings (Dacumos and Rañosa-Madrunio, 2017, p. 49). Manufacturers are required by law to include product warnings in the packaging of cosmetic beauty products. However, compliance to the law does not ensure consumer safety, as reported by the Food and Drug Authority (FDA) of the Philippines. It is in this context that the authors embarked on an analysis of beauty product warnings, specifically focusing on the lexico-syntactic features of product warnings. The hope is that "a data-driven study . . . assessing the correctness and adequacy of safety warnings in consumer products [would lead to] . . . avoiding predictable hazards" (Dacumos and Rañosa-Madrunio, 2017, p. 51). The corpus of the study consisted of forty-five product warnings from beauty products such as baby powder, facial cleanser, facial wash, lotion, lipstick, lip gloss, and press powder. These product warnings were subjected to a frequency count of signal words, concrete and abstract nouns, pronouns, words in field continuum (or vocabulary register), adjectives, and adverbs. Syntax in the product warnings was also analyzed, focusing on conditional sentences and sentence types. The findings point to "the transparency of the communicative features of warning texts" (Dacumos and Rañosa-Madrunio, 2017, p. 66). The findings also reveal the absence of government regulation in standardizing the content of beauty product warnings.

As there were no investigations of beauty product warnings before this study was conducted, this study and the previously mentioned one on household chemical product warnings represent pioneering research. The study also draws attention to lapses in government regulation for beauty product warnings, which were found to lack standard content that may be needed to protect consumers from potential hazards in using the products. It is noted though that the claim about the presence of transparency of the communicative features of warning texts needs more elaboration, as the term *transparency* may also suggest high readability or comprehensibility. There may also be a need to underscore the reality that linguistic features alone may not ensure consumers' protection from hazards, and that the ideal behavior in using the beauty products may also be driven by other factors such as packaging, brand reputation, and so on. In addition, the study is silent on language choice in product warnings, which are most likely formulated in English.

Dacumos and Rañosa-Madrunio (2018) later took a closer look at the comprehensibility of Philippine product warnings by embarking on a study that aimed to address three questions: (1) How do consumer-respondents comprehend existing warning messages? (2) What are the indices of difficulty found in Philippine product warnings? (3) What are the significant reading practices that consumers experience in the course of reading product warnings? and (4) How do these affect their responses to emergency situations? The researchers make the important assumption that product warnings must be readable and comprehensible in language, as well as adequate in content. However, is this really the case for product warnings in the Philippines? To address the questions, forty-seven Filipino mothers were asked to do a cloze test on product warnings for medicines, household chemicals, and beauty products. The participants were also asked to comment on the readability of the product warnings. The findings revealed that product warnings for medicines had the highest number of texts that are considered difficult to read, while beauty products seemed to have the highest number of easy-to-read texts. It is noteworthy that it was stated that easy-to-read texts do not automatically ensure the safety of consumers. This is a recognition that linguistic dimensions alone do not complete the whole picture of product warning uses.

From the perspective of consumers, readability and comprehensibility of information about purchased products are of vital importance. This is even more vital if the products may pose harm to consumers. Cabañas and Rañosa-Madrunio (2020) underscore this in their evaluation of the readability and comprehensibility of patient information leaflets of nonprescription medicines. The corpus of their study consisted of forty-two patient information leaflets (PILs) taken from three common nonprescription medications in Philippine households which include the following categories: (1) fever reducers, (2) cough and cold remedies, and (3) anti-inflammatory drugs. These PILs were subjected to a readability test using the measures of text readability and easability of Coh-metrix. Thereafter, three were randomly selected, each representing one of the medicine categories cited above. These underwent user testing via a cloze procedure followed by forty-one adult participants. The study yielded interesting findings. For example, it was found that based on a readability test, the PILs required high-skilled reading since they were more academic oriented than spoken-like. A user testing of the PILs likewise revealed that less than half of the participants showed an independent level of understanding of the information leaflets. This finding was corroborated by an analysis of the difficulty index of the information content of the PILs. Most of the texts were found to be highly difficult to understand and therefore not suitable for nonspecialist readers. One can surmise that the study is complete in its focal elements. To arrive at those findings, the study employed the tripartite model of communicative effectiveness by Garner and colleagues (2012), which looks into the (1) focus on the text, (2) focus on the text and reader, and (3) focus on the reader. Focusing first on the text (readability) involves analyzing the PILs at the textual/linguistic level. Whereas focus on the text and reader (comprehensibility) allows testing of the users' under-standing of the texts by reacting or interacting with the material, focus on the reader (communicative effectiveness) allows getting feedback from the users as regards their experience in reading the material and how it can be further improved. This is very important, especially given that the end users of the product are healthcare consumers.

It can be deduced that this particular research is unique in the sense that rarely would one find a study in the field of linguistics that makes use of PILs as corpus. Attempting to analyze PILs of nonprescription drugs is a worthy cause as it uncovers the difficulties encountered by the ordinary laypeople who are nonspe-cialist readers in comprehending these texts. The result which revealed that healthcare consumers found the texts of the information leaflets incomprehen-sible is alarming as there already exist healthcare regulatory policies that stand-ardize medical product labels, ensuring accessible medical information. These findings should also raise awareness about drafting these information leaflets using plain language for ordinary healthcare consumers. The authors highly recommend the inclusion of healthcare consumers in the evaluation process and not just experts since the former are the end users of the medicine. Considering that this study is one of the very few to examine consumer products, the study indeed marks a watershed in Philippine FL scholarship. Researchers are thus encouraged to conduct similar studies that have a significant effect on Filipino healthcare consumers to address safety issues, and to promote the general welfare of consumers.

The last set of reviews in this section focused on studies that used corpora close to the everyday lives of the average Filipino. These studies are a welcome addition to both Philippine and international FL research. From consumer finance contracts in the form of CCTC, MOAs signed by collaborating institutions for partnerships to product warnings of hazardous consumer products such as household chemicals and beauty products, and PILs of nonprescription medications in Philippine households, some texts cause uneasiness among ordinary Filipino consumers. Many studies show that most of the respondents who participate in surveys have difficulty comprehending the texts presented to them. Considering that the samples play a vital role in the everyday lives of consumers, these underscore the benefit of using plain language that is simple and easy to understand. The language used by the ordinary Filipino consumer should likewise be given preferential attention to promote the wellbeing of the public. There is no doubt that FL as an area of study can bring about a tremendous change in the many facets of life of Filipinos that were unthinkable in the past.

In this section of the Element, we surveyed developments in FL studies in the Philippines through a critical review of twenty-seven publications in the field. These studies are grouped according to the corpus under study, namely, transcripts of court proceedings, court decisions, public policy/legal provisions, legal contracts, and product warnings/patient information. In the next section, we shall delve into future directions for FL in the Philippines.

4 Charting Future Directions for Forensic Linguistics in the Philippines

The Philippines became officially involved in the new and interesting area of FL just a decade ago. While the term was unknown to most Filipino scholars and researchers, at least four studies have been identified from 1997 to 2012 that used legal documents as corpus for linguistic analysis. Beginning in 2013, FL studies became more widespread in the Philippines, with some branching out into studies on the language of courtroom discourse. Studies that focused on the language of legal documents continued to grow steadily and expand to other legal subgenres.

It should be noted that the studies surveyed in this Element did not follow a set of strict inclusion criteria. Considering that FL is in the stage of infancy in the Philippines, all published studies that investigated language in legal contexts from 2013 onwards were included in this Element. Moreover, four publications that investigated the interface between language and law prior to 2013 were also considered. These four articles, even if they did not make explicit the term *forensic linguistics*, or language and law, have content that focused on language in legal contexts. Thus, they were included in the critical review with the number of studies totaling twenty-seven. Perhaps those studies served as the backbone for future studies from 2013 onwards.

As presented in Table 1 in Section 3, the corpora that received the least amount of attention by Filipino forensic linguists are those that dealt with public policy and legal translation. The number of studies on language in legal processes is noted to be higher than those on the language of legal texts. This does not mean, however, that it is easier to gather corpora or data for investigation when it comes to the courtroom. In fact, in general, it is difficult to gather data from courtroom proceedings because the courtroom is where the operation and practice of law is seen and felt. It is in the courtroom where justice is served and where the protection of rights and freedom is observed. It is also in the courtroom where the institutional ideology of how justice is administered can be displayed. Perhaps it is for these reasons that public policy and legal translation were not common topics or data for investigation as they are not within the bounds of the courtroom.

For studies conducted after 2013, it can be noted that the topics chosen have become more novel, ranging from consumer product warnings, PILs taken from nonprescription medications, territorial disputes, and MOAs. Considering the total numbers of studies included in the critical survey, it can be deduced that in a timespan of less than ten years, there was an effort on the part of some scholars to introduce FL to the country. However, given the figures, more efforts are needed to strengthen FL research in the Philippines. The next ten or twenty years will probably show a different landscape for FL studies as early career researchers become attracted to the field. Research on *language as evidence* should likewise be given equal importance. Similar to courtroom data collection, corpus gathering for this category is an arduous task.

It should be noted that the critical review of the studies conducted revealed that they focused on at least two strands of FL: (1) *the language of the law* and (2) *language as a legal process*. The studies conducted relating to language as a legal process, on the one hand, were directed at courtroom discourse, dealing with the questioning process, court interpreting, and investigative interviewing involving vulnerable and non-vulnerable witnesses. On the other hand, studies on the language of the law consisted of those that concentrated on the use of legalese in consumer contracts and court decisions. These studies recommended the use of plain writing. They likewise highlighted the importance of language comprehensibility in MOAs, public policies in online news articles, PILs, criminal appeal cases, and legal provisions in the real estate industry. While product warnings are not as difficult to comprehend because of the brevity of texts, the said strand was still classified under this category.

From the critical review of twenty-seven studies, we identify several crucial concerns. The first concern is the issue of language policy. Given that FL is a relatively new field of research in applied linguistics in the Philippines, small- and large-scale research at different levels of analysis should be conducted in various parts of the country in order to present a wider and diverse range of cultural, moral, and ethical issues. As mentioned in the earlier parts of this Element, the country is ethno-linguistically diverse, yet language policies relating to law remain English-centric. This is one goal of this review: To strengthen the claim of language scholars that the policy relating to the legal domain should be thoroughly reviewed to make it more inclusive.

It is noteworthy that as the language policy of Philippine courtrooms is reviewed, studies done on FL from 1997 up to the present should be taken into account to validate certain claims and findings. In the Philippines, those who craft language policies are legislators whose field of expertise is detached from language studies or linguistics. Language scholars should be given ample venues of discourse with legislators to lobby such serious concerns. So far, professional organizations meet on a larger scale to consolidate their stances or positions on language issues for more informed and corrected policy-making.

It is also worth noting that more than ten years ago, the country instituted the Mother Tongue Based Multilingual Education (MTB-MLE) policy into the national educational curriculum. Although implementing the policy was found to be very challenging, it remains as the only language policy that is earnest and serious in its claims for upholding inclusivity. Against this back-drop, one hopes that a similar scenario would take place in the legal setting. Whereas the education sector started implementing the said policy more than ten years ago, such is not the case in the legal domain.

In the legal sphere, the official language used is still English, making the litigation process problematic for the poor and the uneducated, putting them at an unfair disadvantage. Even the comprehensibility of legal documents belea-guers the ordinary layperson. In fact, the interplay of power and control is clearly manifested in Philippine courtrooms, where power is wielded by the interrogators who control the public discourse. The threat or use of power by lawyers through their questioning and, at times, offensive tactics coupled with the differences in status between the lawyer and suspects/witnesses make the disadvantaged laypeople become easy prey. Thus, the situation becomes even more serious when societies are multilingual, such as when the language of the court is English and not conveniently absorbed by disadvantaged laypeople

(Rañosa-Madrunio, 2014). Such a concern even extends to suspects and witnesses considered as vulnerable, whose identities should be kept confidential by allowing them to wait in rooms other than the courtroom. At present, many Philippine courtrooms do not have ample space to conduct separate hearings with minors, putting the identity of the vulnerable at stake. With all this happening in Philippine courts, it can be assumed that the Philippine judicial system fails in dispensing true justice to the people. It is no surprise that many Filipinos view the litigation process as threatening, and access to law and justice elusive.

A second concern that can be raised relates to the lack of studies on language as evidence. The critical review of the studies in this Element reveals weaknesses in this particular area of FL. This is symptomatic of weaknesses in criminal investigations, which include subareas such as police investigative interviewing, police reports, hostage-taking negotiations, emergency calls, ransom notes, suicide notes, social media posts, and threat assessment, among others. A study in 2014 by Rañosa Madrunio that took into account linguistic evidence in legal proceedings identified areas of application within the field that are all lacking in FL studies in the Philippines. These are author identification, forensic stylistics, discourse analysis, linguistic dialectology and forensic phonetics, forensic transcription, and language variation. In fact, there is only one study that was critically reviewed in one of these areas authored by Hernandez (2017) on forensic stylistics, which focused on Supreme Court decisions in Philippine English. Even other areas related to FL cited by Ariani and colleagues (2014) such as document examination, software forensics, semiotics, plagiarism detection, and linguists and lawyers' interaction are fertile areas of research as they remain unexplored.

As shown in the foregoing discussion, indeed, much has to be done in the area of FL. As a growing field, FL needs to be further promoted to a wider audience so that young scholars in search of research topics and who are interested in linguistics may find a fertile area to explore. This is true most especially in a country where the delivery of justice needs improvement. Few researchers at this point are well-informed about the convergence of these two disciplines – language and law. As a matter of fact, some have already begun to belittle Filipino researchers, with police officers and lawyers raising questions as to the purpose of these research studies. Having heard of FL for the first time and having almost no background at all on the subject, these stakeholders question the legitimacy of FL studies. In limited instances when they share the data with the FL researchers, they do so with reservations. One can just imagine the level of difficulty FL researchers experience as they go through the investigative process.

A corollary to another weakness mentioned earlier is the lack of studies conducted on language as evidence. Perhaps this is symptomatic of the injustice that many lay Filipinos associate law with. Language as evidence includes the analysis of data such as text messages, suicide notes, death row statements, last will and testaments, ransom notes, obscene phone calls, and many more. Since only a few have trained in the field, it may be argued that many do not see the importance of validating the court's decision through circumstantial evidence, which permits the examination of linguistic features of said forms of textual evidence, most especially when lawyers themselves almost have no awareness of this field. While FL acknowledges that these cannot serve as direct evidence (but are much more than circumstantial evidence), it should be brought to lawyers' attention that by engaging in FL analysis, solving criminal and civil cases can be improved. It should be noted that the current legal system seems closed to linguists doing this kind of analysis for the court, or even for law firms. The dominant mindset remains that only lawyers and legal professionals have the right to conduct research and analyze legal problems and issues. Many believe that lawyers should be placed on a pedestal because they are schooled for a longer period of time than most professionals, and are thereby positioned as authority figures when it comes to legal matters. This is the reason why select academic institutions have decided to offer courses in the undergraduate and graduate programs to facilitate the growth of this emerging field. For those institutions that have become abreast with this new development, some of their students have started working on FL research, most of which have been included in the critical reviews encompassing topics on courtroom discourse, legal contracts, plain language, and police interviewing.

With regard to courtroom hearings, the scenario becomes problematic not only because the language of the legal system in the country is English, which may not be readily comprehensible to some Filipinos due to their diverse linguistic backgrounds, but also because (forensic) linguists are not considered as expert witnesses. To Philippine courts, hiring the services of language specialists/linguists is not a priority; court personnel tend to view linguists as only being engaged in grammar and language styles. Having no knowledge of the existence of FL, court personnel do not see the need to hire the services of FL specialists. Only those in the fields of psychology, medicine, and other science disciplines are called on to be expert witnesses. The inclusion of forensic linguists as expert witnesses will happen only in the next few decades as FL, as an emerging field, reaches a wider audience and becomes ingrained in the legal system. Thus, it is imperative for FL as a discipline to continue to grow so that forensic linguists will gain credibility and be allowed to testify in court.

The critical review of studies done in the preceding section proves that FL has been thriving in the country for the last ten years, yet much still has to be done. For instance, there must be revisions on the rules on expert witnesses in the Rules of Evidence. At present, the Revised Rules of Evidence (2019) makes mention of a handwriting expert in criminal cases, but is silent on language specialists. While it is understood that an expert witness can be any person whose views are accepted by the court by virtue of their education, training, research, skills, and experience, a (forensic) linguist is not one of those invited to render views and opinions on a subject matter. In fact, Section 49 of Rule 130 has been interpreted by the Supreme Court as a firm basis on which the opinion of an expert witness on handwriting may be received in evidence. However, the Supreme Court also made clear that resorting to a handwriting expert is not mandatory and that while it may be useful, handwriting experts are not indispensable in examining or comparing handwriting. The Trial Court is then expected to come to its own conclusion about authenticity based on its own examination of the documents. These rules point to the following inference: that forensic linguists do not have yet a place in Philippine courts. As FL becomes increasingly known in the country, the Rules of Evidence must be amended to include the important role of a forensic linguist in solving crimes.

In addition, it is our hope that FL will also be given importance by law schools so that more research will be conducted in all areas of FL, including research on language as evidence. So far, there is no local research that combines the expertise of linguists, lawyers, legal professionals, and the police. It is hoped that this Element will pave the way for the conceptualization of research on a larger scale, which means involving these professionals, as well as formulating a training design that introduces the police, lawyers, and other legal professionals to the important place of language in legal contexts. Training will prove beneficial, especially to those who, in one way or the other, are involved in the production of legal and courtroom documents such as the court interpreter, court stenographer, and the police. These legal stakeholders need to understand that accuracy in delivering messages may affect legal decisions. Language is not to be taken for granted by courtroom interpreters who enter the field without a sufficient background in translation and interpretation, or even the use of language in general. Professionalizing the field of court interpreters should be considered, and this means requiring that the qualifications of court personnel extend beyond university degrees, and must include training in the language of the law.

Police and courtroom practices should also be reviewed. One area of improvement should be the requirement to record investigative interviews. The interview process should likewise uphold the rights of suspects to opt for the presence of a lawyer, which unfortunately does not happen on a regular basis. Professionalism, training, and the observance of objectivity are key factors in ensuring the success of the interview process. Whereas training calls for regular practice to ensure that high standards are achieved and maintained, professionalism is exemplified by treating the interviewee fairly and in accordance with legislative guidelines. Objectivity is achieved by not allowing personal opinions or beliefs to affect the way in which witnesses, victims, or suspects are dealt with. As for courtroom practices, recorded court proceedings should follow proper storage protocols to allow the court to validate the official transcripts when necessary. In Philippine courtrooms, legal professionals work in a conflict environment where violence and disorder may possibly happen anytime as the conflict is being resolved. However, not enough space is allotted to the witnesses' rooms, especially for the vulnerable who need privacy, as well as security. There is also no provision for police protection of witnesses, except perhaps for those in high-profile cases. These are the most pressing issues that should be attended to as FL becomes a growing field in the Philippines.

This Element on the origins, developments, and directions of FL studies in the Philippines has demonstrated that though in its infancy period, the discipline is alive and well, and its growth is certain. The foundation of FL studies in the country occurred only in 2013, after a small group of Filipino linguists formally trained in the field. The development of FL in the Philippines is a milestone that paves the way for new areas of research intended to help the country improve the delivery of justice. This Element examined the current linguistic landscape of the country, focusing specifically on the legal domain. The Element first presented the language situation in the Philippine legal domain. It then surveyed twenty-seven studies produced from 2013 onwards, including four studies on the interface of language and law prior to 2013. The Element concluded with a discussion of the trajectory of the FL field in the Philippines, as well as an exploration of areas of research that would expand the scope of FL studies in the country. It is hoped that the field of FL will continue to flourish in the country so that concerns about the law and the delivery of justice will account for not only the legal but also the linguistic dimensions of legal practice. And by accounting for the linguistic dimensions, it is also hoped that justice will be better served.

References

Alido, R. A. (2019). The legal provisions in memoranda of agreement (MOA) for academic collaborations: A critical genre analysis (Unpublished PhD dissertation). De La Salle University, Manila.

Andrade, S. M. T., & Ballesteros-Lintao, R. B. (2018). Imposing control through yes/no questions in a Philippine drug trial. *International Journal for the Rule of Law Courtroom Procedures, Judicial Linguistics and Legal English*, *2*(1), 190–230.

Ariani, M. G., Sajedi, F., & Sajedi, M. (2014). Forensic linguistics: A brief overview of the key elements. *Procedia – Social and Behavioral Sciences*, *158*, 222–225. http://dx.doi.org/10.1016/j.sbspro.2014.12.078.

Balgos, A. R. G. (2017). Argumentation in legal discourse: A contrastive analysis of concession in Philippine and American Supreme Court decisions. *Asian Journal of English Language Studies*, *5*, 71–89.

Ballesteros-Lintao, R., & Rañosa-Madrunio, M. (2014). Analyzing the lexical structures of a Philippine consumer finance contract. *Journal of Teaching English for Specific and Academic Purposes*, *2*(3), 359–370.

Ballesteros-Lintao, R., & Rañosa-Madrunio, M. (2015). Status: it's complicated?! Analyzing the comprehensibility of a Philippine consumer-finance contract. *International Journal of Legal English*, *3*(1), 27–45.

Ballesteros-Lintao, R., & Rañosa-Madrunio, M. (2017). Using a holistic and user-centered design in simplifying a Philippine consumer contract. *The Clarity Journal*, *74*, 37–41.

Bhatia, V. K. (1983). Simplification v. easification: The case of legal texts. *Applied Linguistics*, *4*(1), 42–54 https://doi.org/10.1093/applin/4.1.42.

Bhatia, V. K. (2010). Specification in legislative writing: Accessibility, transparency, power and control. In M. Coulthard & A. Johnson (Eds.), *The Routledge handbook of forensic linguistics* (pp. 37–56). Routledge.

Britanico, F. (2022). The courts and testimony of handwriting experts. https://lawyerphilippines.org/the-courts-and-the-testimony-of-handwriting-experts/.

Brylko, A. (2002). Cognitive structuring of criminal appeal cases in Philippine and American English. *Philippine Journal of Linguistics*, *33*(2), 39–51.

Cabañas, A. L. S., & Rañosa-Madrunio, M. (2020). "What's in my medicine?": Evaluating the readability and comprehensibility of patient information leaflets of selected Philippine non-prescription drugs. *Asian Journal of English Language Studies*, *8*, 189–219.

Campbell, N. (2003). Why do banks write the way they do? *The Clarity Journal, 49*, 25–26.

Castro, C. (1997). Cognitive structuring of Philippine criminal appeal cases: An aid to the learner of English for academic legal purposes (EALP). *Teaching English for Specific Purposes, 10*, 85–107.

Cutts, M. (2011). *Plain English lexicon: A guide to whether your words will be understood* (2nd ed.). Plain Language Commission.

Dacumos, S., & Rañosa-Madrunio, M. (2015). The lexical features of Philippine household chemicals' product warnings. *International Journal of Legal English, 3*(2), 31–48.

Dacumos, S., & Rañosa-Madrunio, M. (2017). Lexico-syntactical features of beauty product warnings in the Philippines. *Asian Journal of English Language Studies, 5*, 49–70.

Dacumos, S., & Rañosa-Madrunio, M. (2018). A closer look at the comprehensibility of Philippine product warnings. *The Antoninus Journal, 1*, 1–13.

Del Rosario, V. A. B., & Ballesteros-Lintao, R. B. (2018). Investigative interviewing: Assessing questioning strategies employed to children in conflict with the law. *International Journal of Legal Discourse, 3*(1), 51–76.

Deuna, I. F. G., & Ballesteros-Lintao, R. B. (2022). The language of evaluation in a Philippine drug trial: An appraisal framework perspective. *International Journal of Legal Discourse, 7*(1), 163–193.

Dita, S. N. (2011). The grammar and semantics of adverbial disjuncts in Philippine English. In M. L. S. Bautista (Ed.), *Studies on Philippine English: Exploring the Philippine component of the International Corpus of English* (pp. 33–50). Anvil Publishing for De La Salle University.

Du, J. B. (2016). Staging justice: Courtroom semiotics and the judicial ideology in China. *International Journal for the Semiotics of Law, 29*, 595–614. https://doi.org/10.1007/s11196-015-9444-7.

Eagleson, R. D. (2004). Plain language.gov: Improving communication from the federal government to the public. www.plainlanguage.gov/about/definitions/short-definition.

Felsenfeld, C., & Siegel, A. (1981). *Writing contracts in plain English*. West Publishing.

Finegan, E. (2012). Corpus linguistic approaches to "legal language": Adverbial expression of attitude and emphasis in supreme court opinions. In M. Coulthard, & A. Johnson (Eds.), *The Routledge handbook of forensic linguistics* (pp. 65–76). Routledge.

Garcia-Jawid, M. J. (2009). *What RTC decisions tell us about Philippine culture*. Central Books Supply.

Garner, M., Ning, Z., & Francis, J. (2012). A framework for the evaluation of patient information leaflets. *Health Expectations, 15*(3), 283–294. https://doi.org/10.1111/j.1369-7625.2011.00665.x.

Gibbons, J. (2003). *Forensic linguistics: An introduction to language in the justice system.* Blackwell Publishing.

Gibbons, J. (2004). Taking legal language seriously. In J. Gibbons, V. Prakasam, K. V. Tirumalesh, & H. Nagarajan (Eds.), *Language in the law* (pp. 1–16). Orient Longman Private Limited.

Gibbons, J. (2012). Towards a framework for communication evidence. *The International Journal of Speech, Language and the Law, 18*(2), 233–260.

Gocheco, P. (2007). Legal provisions in the Philippine real estate industry: A genre-based analysis for ESP training. In. C. C. Mann (Ed.), *Current research on applied linguistics* (pp. 101–128). De La Salle University.

Gonzalez, A. (1996). Language and nationalism in the Philippines: An update (1990). In M. L. S. Bautista (Ed.), *Readings in Philippine sociolinguistics* (pp. 228–239). DLSU Press.

Hernandez, H. P. (2017). A (forensic) stylistic analysis of adverbials of attitude and emphasis in supreme court decisions in Philippine English. *Indonesian Journal of Applied Linguistics, 7*(2), 455–466.

Heydon, G. (2019, June 30). Lecture on police investigative interviewing. RMIT University.

Jimenez, R., & Ballesteros-Lintao, R. (2020). A norm-based analysis of court interpretation in selected Philippine criminal cases. *Asian Journal of English Language Studies, 8,* 127–158.

Johnson, A., & Coulthard, M. (2010). Current debates in forensic linguistics. In M. Coulthard & A. Johnson (Eds.), *The Routledge handbook of forensic linguistics* (pp. 1–15). Routledge.

Lewis, M. P., Simons, G. F., & Fennig, C. D. (Eds.). (2016). *Ethnologue: Languages of the world* (19th ed.). SIL International.

Madrilejos, J. I. F., & Ballesteros-Lintao, R. (2020). Interpreting the arguments of China and the Philippines in the South China Sea territorial dispute: A relevance-theoretic perspective. *International Journal for the Semiotics of Law, 35,* 519–564.

Marasigan, M., & Ballesteros-Lintao, R. (2020). Presentation and comprehensibility of public policies in online news articles. *International Journal of Law, Language, and Discourse, 8*(2), 35–56.

Martin, I. P. (2012). Expanding the role of Philippine language in the legal system: The dim prospects. *Asian Perspectives in the Arts and Humanities, 2*(1), 1–14.

Martin, I. P. (2013). Is justice lost in translation? Court interpreting in the Philippines. *Philippine Journal of Linguistics*, *44*, 1–23.

Martin, I. P. (2014). English language teaching in the Philippines. *World Englishes*, *33*(4), 472–485.

Martin, I. P. (2018). Linguistic challenges of an English-dominant legal system in the Philippines. *Asian Englishes*, *20*, 134–146.

Martin, J. R. (2000). Beyond exchange: Appraisal systems in English. In S. Hunston & G. Thompson (Eds.), *Evaluation in text: Authorial stance and the construction of discourse* (pp. 142–175). Oxford University Press.

Martin, J. R. & White, P. (2005). *The language of evaluation*. Palgrave Macmillan.

Pan, Z., & Kosicki, G. M. (1993). Framing analysis: An approach to news discourse. *Political Communication*, *10*, 55–75. https://doi.org/10.1080/10584609.1993.9962963.

Plain Writing for Public Service Act of 2013, S.B. 1092, 16th Congress of the Philippines (2013).

Powell, R. (2012). English in Southeast Asian law. In E. L. Low & A. Hashim (Eds.), *English in Southeast Asia: Features, policy, and language in use* (pp. 241–266). John Benjamins.

Quirk, R., Greenbaum, S., Leech, G., & Svartvik, J. (1985). *A comprehensive grammar of the English language*. Longman Group Limited.

Rañosa-Madrunio, M. (2013). The interrogator and the interrogated: The questioning process in Philippine courtroom discourse. *Philippine Journal of Linguistics*, *43*, 43–60.

Rañosa-Madrunio, M. (2014). Power and control in the Philippine courtroom. *International Journal of Legal English*, *12*(1), 4–30.

Rañosa-Madrunio, M. (2020). Move structure and terms of agreement reflecting legal value in Memoranda of Agreement on academic partnerships. *Philippine Journal of Linguistics*, *51*, 87–113.

Rañosa-Madrunio, M. (2022). Lexical and grammatical features of Memoranda of Agreement (MOA) on academic partnerships. *Journal of English and Applied Linguistics*, *1*(1), 56–78.

Santos, M. V. (2006). A pragmalinguistic analysis of courtroom interrogation in a multilingual context. *The Ateneo de Zamboanga University Journal*, *10*(1), 27–67.

Schuck, P. (1992). Legal complexity: Some causes, consequences and cures. *Duke Law Journal*, *42*(1), 1–52.

Shepherd, E. (2007). *Investigative interviewing: The conversation management approach*. Oxford University Press.

Social Weather Station (SWS). (2005, January 25). New SWS study of the judiciary and the legal profession sees some improvements. www.sws.org.ph/swsmain/artcldisppage/?artcsyscode=ART-20151218115047.

Statista. (2022). Number of reported cases involving illegal drugs in the Philippines in 2021, by region. www.statista.com/statistics/1171104/philippines-crime-incidents-involving-drugs-by-region/. Accessed October 14, 2022.

Tiersma, P. M. (1999). *Legal language*. Chicago University Press.

US Plain English Act of 2010, P.L. 111-274 (2010).

Villanueva, V., & Rañosa-Madrunio, M. (2015). Examining the language in the courtroom interrogation of vulnerable and non-vulnerable witnesses. *Philippine Journal of Linguistics*, *47*, 28–43.

Williams, C. (2011). Legal English and plain language: An update. *ESP Across Cultures*, *8*, 139–151.

Forensic Linguistics

Tim Grant

Aston University

Tim Grant is Professor of Forensic Linguistics, Director of the Aston Institute for Forensic Linguistics, and past president of the International Association of Forensic Linguists. His recent publications have focussed on online sexual abuse conversations including *Language and Online Identities: The Undercover Policing of Internet Sexual Crime* (with Nicci MacLeod, Cambridge, 2020).
Tim is one of the world's most experienced forensic linguistic practitioners and his case work has involved the analysis of abusive and threatening communications in many different contexts including investigations into sexual assault, stalking, murder, and terrorism. He also makes regular media contributions including presenting police appeals such as for the BBC Crimewatch programme.

Tammy Gales

Hofstra University

Tammy Gales is an Associate Professor of Linguistics and the Director of Research at the Institute for Forensic Linguistics, Threat Assessment, and Strategic Analysis at Hofstra University, New York. She has served on the Executive Committee for the International Association of Forensic Linguists (IAFL), is on the editorial board for the peer-reviewed journals *Applied Corpus Linguistics and Language and Law/Linguagem e Direito*, and is a member of the advisory board for the BYU Law and Corpus Linguistics group. Her research interests cross the boundaries of forensic linguistics and language and the law, with a primary focus on threatening communications. She has trained law enforcement agents from agencies across Canada and the U.S. and has applied her work to both criminal and civil cases.

About the Series

Elements in Forensic Linguistics provides high-quality accessible writing, bringing cutting-edge forensic linguistics to students and researchers as well as to practitioners in law enforcement and law. Elements in the series range from descriptive linguistics work, documenting a full range of legal and forensic texts and contexts; empirical findings and methodological developments to enhance research, investigative advice, and evidence for courts; and explorations into the theoretical and ethical foundations of research and practice in forensic linguistics.

Cambridge Elements ≡

Forensic Linguistics

Elements in the Series

A full series listing is available at: www.cambridge.org/EIFL

Printed in the United States
by Baker & Taylor Publisher Services